Native American Myths

Captivating Myths and Legends of Cherooke Mythology, the Choctaws and Other Indigenous Peoples from North America

Free Bonus from Captivating History
(Available for a Limited time)

Hi History Lovers!

Now you have a chance to join our exclusive history list so you can get your first history ebook for free as well as discounts and a potential to get more history books for free! Simply visit the link below to join.

Captivatinghistory.com/ebook

Also, make sure to follow us on Facebook, Twitter and Youtube by searching for Captivating History.

Contents

Part 1: Native American Mythology

Captivating Myths of Indigenous Peoples from North America

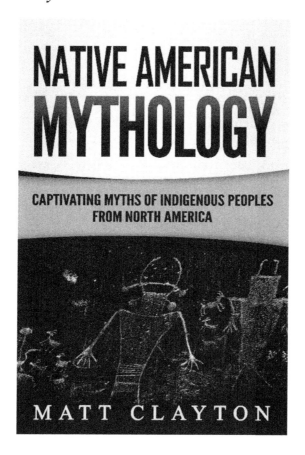

Introduction

Humans have been living and telling their stories in North America since the end of the last Ice Age. The oldest human artifacts found so far seem to date from around 15,000 years ago. Archeologists have long assumed that the first humans crossed the Bering Strait from Asia much earlier than that and then made their way south and east in bands of hunter-gatherers. Today's Indigenous peoples are the descendants of those early explorers.

However, the story of the peopling of the Americas may not be all that straightforward. Author Craig Childs, in his recent book *Atlas of a Lost World*, says that available evidence indicates a much more complicated picture than the simple Bering Strait story would seem to paint. Childs states that there was more than one migration event, that the initial migrations into the Americas likely followed the coastal water routes then available, and that some migrants might have even come from Europe as well as Asia.

Whatever the real story may have been, what followed from the movements of those Ice-Age hunter-gatherer peoples was a great proliferation of cultures and languages. The myriad cultures and societies that lived in North America for thousands of years before the advent of European explorers and colonists developed their own ways of looking at the world and living within the environments they called home. They also developed sophisticated systems of aquaculture, agriculture, hunting, animal husbandry, and land management according to the resources that were available to them.

Part of the history of Indigenous cultures is, of course, their traditions of storytelling. Myths, legends, and folktales all play important roles in explaining how the world came to be the way it is, as well as giving listeners entertainment with humorous or scary stories, or giving them role models to look up to in hero tales. And I use the word "listeners" purposely, for these stories were first transmitted orally, from teller to listener. For the most part, Indigenous peoples did not use writing to record these tales, and with a very few exceptions, no system of writing seems to have existed for Indigenous languages until after the arrival of white missionaries and colonists.

These storytelling traditions are rich indeed, with thousands upon thousands of stories from hundreds of different cultures. Because of this incredible variety, this book provides but the merest sampling of a broad spectrum of myths and legends, and it makes no claim whatsoever to that sample being representative. That said, I have endeavored to provide at least one myth from every major culture group in North America: Arctic, Subarctic, Plateau, Northwest Coast, Great Basin, Great Plains, California, Southwest, Southeast, and Northeast Forest.

Of the many different genres of story available, I have chosen four for this present volume. The first has to do with the origins of things, either of the world in its entirety or some aspect thereof that was significant to the people who created the story. The other side of creation is death, and so the second section concerns tales of ghosts and monsters, some terrifying, some friendly, some the victims of prank-playing living people. However, out of the acts of destruction wrought by supernatural beings there is often something new created or a change worked that is necessary for the world to function properly.

Tricksters and heroes occupy the third and fourth sections of the book, respectively. Coyote is, of course, a favorite trickster character for most North American Indigenous groups, while Raven is important to peoples in the Pacific Northwest and Arctic regions. Beaver is a trickster for the Nez Perce of the Columbia River Plateau, and for the Pomo of California, little Woodrat also lives by his wits. These tricksters are by turns clever, gullible, victor, and victim, but always there is a moral lesson to be learned from the stories of their adventures.

The final section of the book presents stories of Indigenous heroes. Many of these heroes are shared by multiple cultures, usually within the same or adjacent culture areas. Manabozho, the Menominee hero, is honored by the Ojibwe and many other Algonquin-speaking peoples, who know him as Nanabozho or Nanabush. Glooscap is the favorite hero of the Wabanaki peoples of the northeastern United States and Canadian Maritime provinces. Both Manabozho and Glooscap, in addition to doing the usual heroic things such as fighting monsters and working magic, are powerful beings who also are involved in the creation of the world. Other heroes, such as Blood Clot of the Great Basin and the Great Plains, are beings with supernatural origins but are not themselves creator-beings. Not all heroes are powerful supernatural beings, however: the Hunkpapa Brave Woman may have been an actual historical figure.

But the most important thing about all these stories and the many others told by Indigenous peoples is that they are part of an actual living tradition, not part of a dim and misty past of cultures that no longer exist today. This living tradition shows the resilience of Indigenous cultures, which have survived colonization, the introduction of European diseases, the theft of their lands and resources, and outright acts of genocide on the part of white people and their governments. These stories do tell us something about the past of Indigenous peoples, but they are also very much a part of the Indigenous present and hopefully will also be a part of the future.

Part I: Origins

The Cherokee Creation *(Cherokee, Southeast)*

The Cherokee account of how the world was created is an example of what folklorists call an "earth-diver myth." In these types of myths, a creature or being dives down into the primordial waters and brings up a substance that then is transformed into land, which sets the process of creation in motion. The earth-diver in the myths of some tribes is a turtle, while in others it is a muskrat or a water bird. The Cherokee earth-diver is a water beetle, who goes on a quest on behalf of the other creatures to bring up the bit of mud that becomes the earth.

Whereas in European creation myths a deity or group of deities create the world by the exercise of their power or will, in the Cherokee account the process of creation is begun by the creatures themselves. Insects, animals, and birds all work in concert with the Great Spirit to shape the world and bring it to life, including correcting the Great Spirit's mistake of having placed the sun too close to the ground. Unlike the animals and birds, who existed prior to the world itself, human beings are newcomers and must be created out of nothing by the Great Spirit.

Once there was a time when there was no earth at all. Everything was covered with water, and all the creatures lived in Galunlati, a place that is above the sky. Galunlati was a pleasant place, but soon it became very crowded, and the creatures were unhappy.

"What shall we do?" said the creatures. "There are so many of us, we can barely move."

"I know!" said one of them. "Let's ask Water Beetle to go into the water below and see what he can do about this."

Water Beetle agreed to this plan. He left Galunlati and dove into the waters. He swam around for a bit but didn't see anything that looked like a good place to live, so then he dove deeper. Down, down, down he went, to the bottom of the sea. He picked up a bit of mud in his jaws and brought it up to the surface. When Water Beetle reached the surface with the mud, the mud began to spread out in all directions. The spread-out mud became an island, and the Great Spirit secured it by using cords to tie it to the vault of the sky.

Now, this new island was very good, and it was quite secure, but the ground was too soft for most of the creatures to live on. The creatures decided to send Buzzard down to see whether he might do anything to fix that. Buzzard flew around and around but didn't find anywhere dry enough to land. He flew around some more and finally found one spot that was just dry enough for him to land on. The place where Buzzard landed became the home of the Cherokees, and the flapping of Buzzard's wings as he was landing pushed up the mud in some places and pushed it down in others, forming the hills and mountains and valleys of the world.

Finally the new earth was dry enough for all the creatures to walk on. They came down from the sky vault and looked around their new home. It was solid enough, but it was very dark. The creatures didn't like the darkness, so they invited Sun to come down and join them. She came and agreed to walk a particular path every day to give light to the new world.

Everyone except Crawfish was happy about the light Sun gave. It was much too hot for him. "Look at my beautiful shell!" he cried. "Look! It's turned bright red because Sun is too hot. Can anyone help me?"

The creatures took pity on Crawfish and raised Sun a little higher. It was still too hot. So they raised Sun a bit more. It was still too hot. Seven times they pushed Sun a little farther up in the sky. After the seventh time, Sun was finally in the right spot.

Now that there was land and water and light, the Great Spirit decided to make plants to grow on the new land. When all the plants were made, he told them and all the animals that they should stay awake for seven whole days. The animals tried their best, but the only one who was able to stay awake the whole time was Owl. Because he succeeded, the Great Spirit gave Owl the power of seeing in the dark. The plants also tried, but only the pines, firs, holly, and some others were able to stay awake the whole time. The Great Spirit gave them the gift of keeping their leaves all year round.

Once all the plants were made, the Great Spirit decided that there should be people in the world. The Great Spirit made a man and a woman. When man and woman were first created, they did not know how to make children in the usual way. The first time they made children, the man took a fish and pushed it against the woman's belly. Then the woman gave birth to a child. They did this every seven days. After the seventh day, the Great Spirit thought that that was enough for now, and he made it so that women could only have a child once a year.

The Good Twin and the Evil Twin *(Yuma, Southwest)*

The creation myth of the Yuma people of Arizona is very different from the Cherokee story. In the Yuma account, the creator is a supernatural dual being, having good and evil aspects. This being arises out of the primordial waters in its good aspect first, and when the evil aspect tries to rise, the good aspect ensures that it is blinded in order to limit its power.

This version of the myth was collected after the advent of Europeans into Yuma territory. The Yuma creation story not only explains how people came to be but also attributes the creation of separate cultures to Kokomaht, the All-Father who is the primary creator of the world. Once the Yuma encountered white people, they apparently thought it necessary to incorporate them into their creation myth.

What the Yuma have to say about Europeans is not flattering, and considering the history of the behavior of whites toward Indigenous peoples, this is neither surprising nor unreasonable. The white people that figure in this story are painted as selfish, greedy, vain, and petulant, and as interlopers unfit for survival in the desert environment that the Yuma inhabit, the environment for which the Yuma believe they were specially made by Kokomaht.

In the very beginning, the only thing in existence was water. The sky had not yet been made. The earth had not yet been made. There were no plants or animals or fish or people. The sky was made when the waters swirled and swirled about and made foam and spray. The foam and spray rose up, up, up, and turned into the sky.

Down at the very bottom of the waters, there was a being that was one and two at the same time, and the two were twins. The being's name was Kokomaht, which means All-Father.

A second time the waters swirled about. They crashed and thundered in great waves. Again the crashing and swirling of the waters made foam and spray. Up from the depths a being arose. It rose up through the waters with its eyes closed and pushed through the surface. Then it stood upon the surface of the waters and looked about. The being called itself Kokomaht, and Kokomaht was a good being.

As Kokomaht looked over the waters and up in the sky, he heard a voice calling to him from the depths. The voice said, "My brother! When you rose to the surface, did you keep your eyes open or closed?"

Now, Kokomaht knew that the voice belonged to his brother, and that his brother had an evil nature. Kokomaht wanted to make sure that his brother could work as little evil as possible, so he lied and said, "Oh, I kept my eyes open the whole way!"

The evil twin believed what Kokomaht said. He kept his eyes open as he rose to the surface, but in doing so, he blinded himself. Kokomaht named his twin "Bakotahl," which means "Blind One."

Kokomaht decided that it was time to create the earth. First, he created the four directions. He took four steps in one direction, stopped, pointed in the direction he had been going, and then said, "This is north." Then he went back to the center again. Kokomaht turned around and went the opposite way. He took four steps, pointed, and said, "This is south." He returned to the center, and in the same way he created east and west.

"It is now time to make the earth," said Kokomaht, but Bakotahl objected.

"I should be the one to make the earth," said Bakotahl.

"No, I am going to do it," said Kokomaht, and so he put his hand into the waters and began stirring. Kokomaht stirred and stirred the waters, and soon they became so agitated that a great mass of land came to the surface. Kokomaht went onto the new land and sat down.

Bakotahl was angry and envious that his brother got to make the earth, but he kept his feelings to himself. Bakotahl also climbed onto the new land and sat down next to Kokomaht. Bakotahl thought to himself, "If I am not to be allowed to make the land, then I shall make some people to live on it."

Bakotahl took up a handful of mud and started forming it into a creature. Bakotahl gave the creature a head and a body. He gave it arms and legs. But he forgot to put fingers and toes on the hands. Bakotahl's new creature was lumpy and imperfect, and so Bakotahl was ashamed of it and hid it from his brother.

Kokomaht then said, "I think I shall make some people to walk on this new land." Kokomaht took up a handful of mud and shaped it into a being. He gave it a head and a body. He gave it arms and legs. He put fingers and toes on the hands and feet, and gave the being a beautiful face. Everything about Kokomaht's new being was perfect.

When the being was all made, Kokomaht took it and waved it four times toward the north. Kokomaht then set the new being down upon the new land, and the being came alive. It stood on its feet and walked around. It could see and hear and taste and smell. This being was the first man. Then Kokomaht took up another handful of mud and made a woman the same way he had made the man.

Bakotahl made another attempt at making people. When he had made seven of his lumpy, imperfect creatures, Kokomaht asked him what he was making.

"I am making people," said Bakotahl.

"Hm," said Kokomaht. "I think they're missing some important things. Here, feel the people I made. They have fingers and toes and features on their faces. Yours are lumpy and misshapen. They won't be able to care for themselves or each other." Then Kokomaht took his foot and kicked Bakotahl's new beings into the water.

When Bakotahl learned what Kokomaht had done, he became terribly angry. Bakotahl dove into the water and swam down, down, down into the depths. Bakotahl made the waters swirl and heave, and up out of the depths he sent a whirlwind. Kokomaht saw the whirlwind, and when it got near enough, he stepped on it and crushed it to death. But not all of the whirlwind was crushed; one little piece escaped from beneath Kokomaht's foot, and this is where all sicknesses come from.

Now all there was on the new land was Kokomaht and the new man and the new woman, and they were the first Yumas. Kokomaht made more men and more women. He put them in pairs, and each pair became the first ones of new tribes, the Cocopahs, Digueños, and Mojaves. Now that Kokomaht had made four pairs of people, he rested a while. When he was done with his rest, Kokomaht made the first men and first women for the Apaches, the Maricopas, the Pimas, and the Coahuilas. In this way, Kokomaht made the first men and first women for twenty-four tribes of people. The white people were the last ones he made.

The Yuma man said to Kokomaht, "We don't know how to live in this new place. Please teach us."

"First you must learn about children," said Kokomaht, and so he made a son for himself and called him Komashtam'ho. Then Kokomaht said to the people, "Men and women should live together and have children together."

Kokomaht looked at the sky and the land and the people he had made. These were all good things, but he felt that his creation was incomplete. "I know!" said Kokomaht. "My new people will need light."

Kokomaht then created the moon and the morning star. Then he made all the other stars that shine at night. When this was done, Kokomaht looked at all the new things he had made and said, "I think I have created enough. My son can make more new things if he wants to."

In addition to the land and the people and the moon and the stars, Kokomaht had created some other beings. One of these was Hanyi, the Frog. Hanyi was very jealous of Kokomaht's power and would have liked nothing better than to destroy him. Of course Kokomaht knew what was in Hanyi's heart because he knew the thoughts of all the beings he created. Kokomaht thought, "I have one last lesson to teach my new beings, and I will have Hanyi help me. I must teach the people how to die. I will let Hanyi kill me."

Hanyi decided the time had come for her to try to kill Kokomaht. She burrowed into the earth beneath Kokomaht's feet and sucked all his breath out through a hole in the earth that was there. When Hanyi had taken all of Kokomaht's breath, Kokomaht became very sick. He lay down on the earth. He called all the new people he had made to come and watch how to die. Everyone came except the white man. He stayed in his own country in the west of the world.

Now, the white man was very unhappy and dissatisfied with everything. He was also very greedy, taking what didn't belong to him without asking. One day, the white man sat crying because he didn't like his curly, pale hair and pale skin. Komashtam'ho was tired of listening to the white man feeling sorry for himself, so he took two sticks and tied them together into a cross. He gave the sticks to the white man. "Here," said Komashtam'ho. "Take these. You can ride on them. Just stop whining." The white man took the sticks and straddled them. The sticks turned into a horse, and for a while the white man stopped crying and complaining.

Kokomaht lay on the ground, where he was deathly ill. He said to the people, "This is the last thing I will teach you. I will teach you how to die." After he finished speaking, Kokomaht died.

When Kokomaht was dead, Komashtam'ho began to think of what he would like to create for this new world his father had made. He thought that maybe it would be good to have both night and day, so he spat into his hand and made a disk out of the spittle. Komashtam'ho took the disk and threw it into the east, where it began to shine. Now the world had a sun as well as a moon and stars.

Komashtam'ho explained to the people that the sun would move from east to west and that there now would be day and night. To show them how this would be, he took the sun and pushed it under the earth, making everything dark again. While it was dark, Komashtam'ho made some more stars and put them into the sky. "When the sun is out, it will be day, and there will be much light. You will not be able to see the stars. When the sun sets in the west, it will be night, and it will be dark again. You will be able to see the stars."

When the sun had been made, Komashtam'ho thought about what he should do with his father's body. He decided that the best thing would be to burn it on a pyre, but there was nothing on the new earth that would burn, so Komashtam'ho made wood. He heaped the wood into a large pyre and put his father's body on top of it.

Now, Komashtam'ho knew that Coyote was likely to try some kind of a trick with his father's body, so he gave Coyote a stick and told him to go fetch fire from the sun. When Coyote had run away, Komashtam'ho showed the people how to make their own fire using a piece of wood with a hole in it and another stick. Komashtam'ho put one end of the stick into the hole and twirled it between his hands until a small flame licked up. This is how the people learned how to make fire. Then Komashtam'ho took the flame and used it to light the funeral pyre.

The people all gathered around the pyre and watched it burn, but they did not mourn for Kokomaht because they didn't yet understand that death was forever. As the pyre was beginning to burn, Coyote returned. He jumped over all the people onto the pyre, where he took the heart of Kokomaht in his jaws and ate it before running away.

Komashtam'ho was very angry at Coyote. "You will be cursed for that!" he shouted. "You will always live in the wilderness, and you will be a thief. Everyone will shun you and kill you when they can."

Then Komashtam'ho turned to the people and said, "Now you know about death. Kokomaht will never be among you ever again, for death must be for always. If there was no death, there would be too many creatures in the world, and there wouldn't be enough food."

When the people heard that Kokomaht would never return, they began to weep, for now they understood that death was for always. And because the flames of Kokomaht's pyre were so very hot, it made the whole land hot ever after. Hanyi the Frog watched the people mourning for Kokomaht and understood that they would be very angry with her for killing him. So Hanyi buried herself in a burrow underground, and that is why frogs still live in those burrows to this day.

Komashtam'ho saw the people weeping, and he said to them, "You will mourn now, and that is fitting, but when you die, your spirits will go to the place where Kokomaht is. There you will always be happy, as he is happy now."

Then Komashtam'ho decided he needed help with creating the rest of the world. He chose a man named Marhokuvek to help him. Marhokuvek looked at the people and creatures mourning for Kokomaht and saw that they were all covered with long hair, for people and animals and birds did not look all that different from one another when the world was first made. Marhokuvek said, "Let us cut our hair as a sign that we are in mourning."

The people and animals and birds thought this was a good idea, and so they cut off all their hair, but when Komashtam'ho saw what the animals and birds looked like without their hair, he said, "The people look all right without hair, but the animals and birds do not." So Komashtam'ho changed the forms of the animals and birds into the shapes they have now, and gave hair to the animals and feathers to the birds. Then Komashtam'ho realized that some of the animals and birds were very wild and dangerous indeed, so he sent a great rain to wash these away. It rained and it rained and it rained, and soon the whole world was flooding. The flood washed away many of the dangerous animals, but it also began to kill some of the good animals and people as well, and the air became very cold.

"Please stop the flood!" said Marhokuvek. "You are killing people and good animals, and the people cannot live in such a cold world!"

Komashtam'ho agreed to stop the rain, but from that day forward, the animals, birds, and people lived separately, and the animals and birds were afraid of the people. To dry up all the floodwaters, Komashtam'ho kindled a great fire, which burned all the land. This is why the home of the Yuma people is a desert.

Now, the body of Kokomaht had been well destroyed in the flames, but his house was still standing, with all his belongings inside. Komashtam'ho said to the people, "We shouldn't leave Kokomaht's house standing because he is dead now, and every time we see his house or his belongings, it will make us sad. So when someone dies, we have to destroy their house and their belongings."

Komashtam'ho went to his father's house and used a long pole to knock it down. Then he used the pole to dig up the place where the house had been. Water began to well up from the ground in the places that Komashtam'ho had dug into the soil, and the grooves made by the pole filled with the water and became the Colorado River.

Now, the people that Bakotahl had made had not been completely destroyed. They still lived, although they had neither hands nor feet, nor fingers nor toes. Some of these beings became the fish and other creatures who live in the water, while others turned into waterfowl.

After all had been created, the different kinds of people parted from one another and went to live in different places. Komashtam'ho said to the Yuma people, "I have finished creating the world. I will always be with you, but I must change my form because I will also need to be with other people as well. And in my new form, you must call me by a new name. I shall be Eshpahkomahl, the White Eagle."

Then Komashtam'ho changed himself into four eagles. One was black and flew to the west; this is where dark clouds and rain come from. One was brown and went to the south and flew over the rivers to catch fish. No one knows what the third eagle looks like, for no one has ever seen him. Komashtam'ho himself flew to the north in the form of a white eagle.

And Bakotahl? He still lives under the earth and still has an evil heart. Sometimes the earth shakes, and the people say that it is Bakotahl moving about in his underground home.

Pushing up the Sky *(Snohomish, Northwest Coast)*

The Snohomish people of Puget Sound acknowledge a single creator who makes the world, and although the creator does a good job, he neglects to make the sky high enough, so the people and animals have to fix the problem. This legend therefore functions as a just-so story about why the sky is so far away and about why it is so difficult to get into the Sky World, a mythical region above the earth that contains the stars.

According to the Snohomish myth, in the beginning it was easy for people and animals to go into the Sky World because the sky was so low and actually touched the earth at the horizon. The permeable nature of the earth/sky boundary factors into another just-so aspect of this tale, which explains the origin of the constellations of the Big and Little Dippers. These two constellations are formed when some hunters and fishermen accidentally cross the earth/sky boundary during the sky-pushing and end up caught in the Sky World, where they turn into stars.

The retelling below is based on a version of the legend told by Snohomish Chief William Shelton.

The Creator and Changer made the whole world. He started in the east and worked his way westward. He created the land and the waters, the birds and the beasts, and the people. He gave all the creatures their places to live, and he gave languages to the people. When he had made the land from the east all the way to Puget Sound, and when he had put all the people and all the creatures in their places, he saw that he still had many, many languages left to give. So he scattered them all around Puget Sound and the lands to the north, and so it was that the people who lived in that part of the world spoke many, many different languages and could not always understand one another.

The people all had good places to live, but there was one thing about the world they did not like. The Creator hadn't put the sky up high enough, and the tall people were always bumping their heads on it. There was also a second problem: if a person climbed high enough into a tall tree, they could enter the Sky World, and they often didn't come back.

Finally the elders of the tribes got together to see whether they could figure out what to do about the sky being so low. After talking for a long time, they agreed that somehow they needed to push the sky up higher.

"This will take all of us working together," said one very wise elder. "All the people and all the birds and all the animals will have to push at the same time."

"This is a good plan," said another elder, "but how will we make sure everyone works together like that? We speak too many languages, and we need one signal everyone will understand."

"I know what we can do!" said a third elder. "Let's all push when someone shouts 'Ya-hoh.' That word is the same in all our languages, and it means 'let's push together.'"

The elders all agreed that this was a very good plan. They sent messengers throughout the whole land, telling the people and the birds and the animals what they were going to do, and setting a day for them to push up the sky. The messengers also told the people to take the trunks of fir trees and fit them to use as poles to push the sky up.

The people worked very hard making the poles. Finally the day to push up the sky arrived. The people raised their poles, set them against the sky, and got ready to push. When everyone was in place, the elders all cried, "Ya-hoh!" and the people pushed on the sky with their poles. The sky moved a little bit. So, the elders cried, "Ya-hoh!" again, and the people pushed again, and the sky moved up a little bit more. The people worked and worked this way for a long time. The elders would cry, "Ya-hoh!" and everyone would push, and finally, after much effort, they had put the sky where it is now. The tall people were much happier because they were no longer bumping their heads all the time. And since the day of the sky-pushing, no one has been able to climb high enough to get into the Sky World.

Now, not everyone had heard about the sky-pushing. There were three hunters who had been out chasing four elk and so were away from the rest of the people when the messengers came. They chased and chased the elk for several days. On the day set for the sky-pushing but before the people had begun their work with their poles, the hunters and their prey came to the place where the sky met the earth. The elk jumped into the Sky World, and the hunters followed them, but when the people lifted up the sky, the elk and the hunters went up with it, along with their dog.

The elk, the dog, and the hunters could not leave the Sky World, and there they turned into stars. You can still see them there even today. The three hunters form the handle of the Big Dipper, and you can see the dog as a very small star next to the bigger one in the middle of the handle. The elk form the bowl of the Big Dipper.

The hunters were not the only ones that got caught in the sky that day. There were two canoes with three fishermen each that were out fishing. They got caught up in the sky when it lifted, too, along with a fish, and they also were all turned into stars, and became the Little Dipper.

And to this day, the people who live in Puget Sound still shout "Ya-hoh!" when they have to do a difficult task together.

The Origin of El Capitan *(Miwok, California)*

El Capitan is an enormous granite monolith on the north side of the Yosemite Valley in California. In this story of how El Capitan came to be, told by the Miwok people of central California, there is no direct action by a supernatural being, just a random occurrence that results in an otherwise unremarkable large, flat rock suddenly growing overnight into something the size of a mountain.

One of the primary features of El Capitan is the nearly sheer vertical surface of its face, which is scalable only by a few of the most skilled climbers. The difficulty inherent in climbing El Capitan therefore figures largely in this story, which begins when a family of bears is stranded at the top of the monolith when it grows under them during the night. As soon as the other animals discover what has happened to the bears, they rush to launch a rescue mission to get the bears down. However, none of the animals are able to climb very high up the cliff face, no matter how hard they try, until finally the lowly inchworm, who can cling to just about anything, offers to go. The inchworm does make it to the top, but not before the bears have died from starvation.

The sheerness of the cliff face and the idea that nothing but a clingy worm might be able to climb it factors into the Miwok name for El Capitan: Tutokanula, *or "Inchworm Stone."*

There was a time when a mother bear and her two cubs spent the day along the Merced River looking for food. They had walked and foraged for a very long time, and they were very tired. They walked a little farther, looking for a place to rest. Soon they came upon a large, flat rock that was big enough for all of them to lie down on. The bears climbed up on the rock, curled up, and went to sleep.

The bears slept soundly on the rock all night. They slept so soundly that they did not notice the rock growing and growing under them while they slept. The rock grew so much, that when the bears woke in the morning, they found they could touch the moon. The bears were very frightened. They looked over the edge of the rock. All they saw was the sheer edge of the cliff face. No matter which way they looked, they could not find a way back down to the valley.

The bears were not the only ones who were surprised by what happened. The birds and animals of the Yosemite Valley looked up in shock when they found that the flat rock at the side of the river was now as big as a mountain. The birds and animals also heard the cries of the mother bear and her cubs, and they saw the bears peering cautiously over the edge of the great rock.

All the animals and birds were very worried about the bear and her cubs. "How are we to get them down?" they said. "There's no food up there. If we don't rescue those bears, they will starve!"

So the animals and birds came together in a great council to determine what was to be done. In the end, they decided that someone needed to climb up to the bears and help them get down.

"I'll go!" said Mouse, and he scampered off to the rescue. But try as he might, little Mouse was unable to climb very far up the steep sides of the giant rock.

Next Rat said that he would go, but he had no more success than Mouse had done, although he was able to climb just a bit higher. Rabbit went next and got a little higher than Rat had done, but he came nowhere near the top. Then Mountain Lion tried, and Fox, and Crow, and many other creatures after them, but none of them were able to climb high enough to help the bears.

Soon all the animals and birds despaired of being able to help the bears. Finally, little Inchworm came forward. "I may be very small," he said, "but I'm a very good climber."

And so Inchworm inched off to the foot of the great rock and began to climb. Slowly and carefully he made his way up the steep face of the cliff. He passed the place where Mouse had had to stop. Then he passed the place that Rat had reached. Then he passed the places that Mountain Lion, Fox, and Crow had reached. Soon Inchworm had passed the places that all the other animals had been able to climb to, and still he kept climbing on and on.

It took a very long time for Inchworm to reach the top of the huge cliff, but finally he arrived. Unfortunately, because it had taken so long for anyone to come to the rescue, the bears had starved to death by the time Inchworm arrived. Inchworm gathered up the bones and brought them down to where the other animals were waiting. Everyone was very sad that the bears had died, and they put the bones to rest in the traditional way.

And this is why the mountain that white people call "El Capitan" is called "Tutokanula" by the Miwoks, because that word means "Inchworm Stone" in their language.

Part II: Ghosts and Monsters

Burnt-Stick and the Wendigo *(Sweet Grass Cree, Subarctic)*

The wendigo is a fearsome two-faced giant with a taste for human flesh who appears in stories from Algonquin and Dene tribes. In this story from the Sweet Grass Cree of Saskatchewan, Canada, we learn that the wendigo is so dangerous that even Wisahketchahk, the main Algonquin culture hero, is afraid of it.

Here a girl named Burnt-Stick comes to live with eleven brothers who have escaped the wendigo and who are also accompanied by Wisahketchahk. But Burnt-Stick is no ordinary girl; from the very moment of her arrival, it is clear she has supernatural origins. Her capture by the wendigo—which she escapes with the help of the creature's grandmother—is what eventually leads to the wendigo being soundly killed by a young man who also seems to be a supernatural being.

Burnt-Stick lives with the young man and his wife for a time, and there she assumes male clothing and goes hunting as though she were a man. This cross-dressing later saves her from being pounced on by an evil man who likes to dive out of trees onto unsuspecting women to maim or kill them. Of course Burnt-Stick goes on to give the evil man his just deserts, and returns to her brothers with some of the young women she saved to be their wives, thus undoing some of the wendigo's evil by making it possible to increase the population.

The retelling presented below is based on the story told by the Cree storyteller Louis Moosimin to Canadian anthropologist Leonard Bloomfield in the early 20th century.

Once there was a dreadful wendigo who had made it his task to destroy every human being in the world. He attacked encampment after encampment, killing and eating as many people as he could. After one attack, ten young men managed to escape together. When the wendigo found out they had escaped, he chased after them, but they always managed to find a new place to camp and to leave before the wendigo could catch them.

The young men had fled so quickly that they had left their little brother behind. They went back to get their little brother and then moved on. The young men and their little brother found a good place to set up their encampment. It was a good place that seemed safe from the wendigo. While the elder brothers did the hunting and other tasks that men do, the younger brother stayed in the lodge and did things like tend the fire.

One day, as the younger brother was tending the fire, he stepped on a piece of wood. He found that a splinter had pierced the skin of his sole. The young boy pulled the splinter out of his foot and then threw it out the door of the lodge. No sooner had he done that than a little girl-child came crawling in. "Oh no you don't," said the young boy. "I don't know how to take care of a girl, and neither do my brothers." And so he took the girl-child and put her back outside the lodge.

Not a moment later, the girl-child came back in. She was much bigger than she had been before, but again the young boy put her back outside. Another time the girl came in, and this time she looked at the boy and said, "Big brother!" to him. The boy set her outside yet again, thinking to himself, "Maybe when she comes back next time, she will be all grown up. If she has been sent to us by the spirits, then she will be grown up, and she can stay with us."

Sure enough, the girl came back, and this time she had grown into a young woman. "Come in and sit down, Big Sister!" said the young boy, and so she came into the lodge. The young boy gave her the name Burnt-Stick. The boy introduced Burnt-Stick to his brothers, and they were glad to have her join them to do the work that women usually do.

Now, at this time, Wisahketchahk was also staying with the ten young men, and he was with them because he was terribly frightened. The wendigo was such a fearsome beast that even Wisahketchahk ran from him. Wisahketchahk stayed with the young men because they knew much about the ways of the wendigo, how it hunted and which paths it walked. When Wisahketchahk met Burnt-Stick, he said, "Welcome, Little Sister!" and it was then that the young men and their little brother knew that it was right for Burnt-Stick to stay with them.

And so this little band lived together and worked together. The men hunted and fished and did all the work that men usually do, while Burnt-Stick tanned hides and sewed clothing and cooked and did all the work that women usually do, and for a time they were all very happy together in that place.

One day, Wisahketchahk said to Burnt-Stick, "We have been here for some time. The wendigo probably knows where we are. But your brothers and I need to go away for a few days, and you must stay here by yourself. If you do what I tell you, you will be safe.

"First, you must go out and collect enough firewood to last you four nights. Whenever you are gathering firewood from now on, do not pick up anything else but the wood. While we are not at home, you might hear someone calling to you, but you must not answer. For the four nights we will be away, it will be very cold. You might hear what sounds like our voices outside the lodge, but it will not be us. You must stay inside and not open the door. The wendigo is sure to be abroad while we are away, and he has such great power that even I am afraid of him."

The young woman followed Wisahketchahk's advice. She went into the forest and gathered a lot of wood for the fire. She also cut down a tree and split the wood to use as well. She put all the firewood inside the lodge and sealed the door because the weather had become very, very cold.

After a little while, she heard someone say, "Little Sister, we have returned!" but Burnt-Stick remembered what Wisahketchahk had told her. She didn't answer, and she didn't open the door. Then she heard what sounded like her brothers suffering from the cold. "We are dying!" the voices said. "We are dying from the cold! Open the door, and let us in!" Burnt-Stick didn't open the door, and in the morning when she went outside, there were no footprints at all. "Wisahketchahk was right!" she thought. "The wendigo did come last night, and he tried to trick me!"

After four nights, the men came back to the lodge. Burnt-Stick had followed Wisahketchahk's instructions and had stayed safe the whole time. The morning after the men came home, Burnt-Stick went to collect wood for the fire. But this time she forgot Wisahketchahk's warning, and she picked up a pretty feather she found on the forest floor. Suddenly, the wendigo came out of the feather, saying, "Aha! I have you at last. You are young and tender, and you shall make a tasty dish for me when you have been properly fattened." Then the wendigo picked up Burnt-Stick, threw her over his shoulder, and strode back to his home.

Now, the wendigo lived with his old grandmother, and it was she who cooked the people that he brought home to eat. When the wendigo arrived home with Burnt-Stick, he put the girl down and said, "Hey, Grandmother! Look at this tasty morsel I found. Fatten her up nicely for me, for I intend to feast on her when she is ready."

For a time Burnt-Stick lived with the wendigo and his grandmother. Then came the day when the wendigo decided that he would eat Burnt-Stick. He told his grandmother to kill the girl and cook her, and then he went out.

The grandmother did not want to kill Burnt-Stick because she had become fond of the young girl. The grandmother went to Burnt-Stick and said, "Grandchild, the wendigo wants me to kill you so that he can eat you, but I don't want to do that. I have already had a long life; take that axe there, and kill me by striking me in the head with it, and then put me in the pot instead. When you have done that, run far away from here. Go in that direction when you leave. You will see four hills in front of you. You must climb each one of those. When you have crossed the hills, you will find an iron house. Knock on the door of that house, and ask for help. The one who lives there can kill the wendigo. Say to the one who lives there, 'Big Brother! Help me! The wendigo wants to eat me!' and then you will have good help."

When the grandmother was done instructing Burnt-Stick, the young woman took the axe and killed her. Then she skinned the grandmother, cut her up, and set her in a kettle over the stove to cook. As soon as the meal was done cooking, Burnt-Stick ran out of the wendigo's house in the direction the grandmother had told her to go. Burnt-Stick came across the first hill. She climbed up one side and down the other. Then she came to the second hill, and she climbed that one as well. But as she began to climb the third hill, she heard the roaring voice of the wendigo behind her. The wendigo had discovered that he had eaten his grandmother instead of having eaten Burnt-Stick, and he was very angry. "You will never get away from me!" roared the wendigo. "I will follow you everywhere, and I will surely find you and eat you!"

Burnt-Stick began to run even faster. She went down the third hill and climbed up the fourth. As she crested that hill, she looked behind her, and there in the distance was the wendigo, running as fast as he could to catch her. Then Burnt-Stick looked down in front of her, and there was the iron house as the grandmother had told her. She ran as fast as she could and then began pounding on the door and shouting, "Please, oh please let me in! The wendigo is chasing me!"

But these were not the words the grandmother had told Burnt-Stick to use, so the people inside the house did not open the door. Finally Burnt-Stick remembered what she had to say. "Big Brother! Help me! The wendigo wants to eat me!"

As soon as Burnt-Stick said those words, the door opened, and she went inside the house. Inside there were a young man and a young woman. The young woman said to Burnt-Stick, "Sister-in-law, welcome! Please come sit down!"

No sooner had Burnt-Stick sat down than they heard the wendigo roaring its way around the house. "Open this door!" screamed the wendigo. "Open this door, and let me in! I mean to have that girl for my dinner! Open up!"

The young man took up his axe and opened the door. As soon as the wendigo stuck its head in, the young man swung the axe and chopped off the wendigo's head.

The young man and young woman welcomed Burnt-Stick into their home. She lived with them for some time. The young man and young woman made a talisman for Burnt-Stick to carry with her. "This will give you manitou power," they said. They also made men's clothing for Burnt-Stick to wear, and dressed as a man, she went out hunting every day.

One day, the young man and young woman said to Burnt-Stick, "Your brothers miss you. You really should go visit them. But on your way home, take care; there is an evil man who lives in a huge tipi. He likes to climb up into trees and jump down upon the people who pass by. Every time he lands on someone, he breaks their bones. Sometimes he even kills them. Now, he will not try to kill you if you are dressed like a man; he only jumps on women. But maybe you can do something about that evil man when you come across him."

Burnt-Stick began her journey homeward. She tried to avoid the evil man's camp, but he had seen her approaching from afar and met her on the trail. Thinking Burnt-Stick was a man, the evil one said, "Come and enjoy hospitality at my lodge." Burnt-Stick couldn't refuse for fear of raising his suspicions.

They walked on for a time, and slowly it dawned on the evil man that Burnt-Stick was, in fact, a woman and not a man. He made a plan to jump on her out of a tree but not before he had frightened her by showing her all the young women whose bones he had broken whom he forced to live with him. Burnt-Stick sensed that the evil man had discovered who she really was, so she picked up a long piece of saskatoon wood and pretended she needed it for a walking stick.

The evil man led Burnt-Stick into his lodge, and there she saw the broken bodies of all the women he had harmed. Burnt-Stick felt sorrow and anger for them, and she vowed to stop the evil man from hurting anyone else.

"Come and sit here," said the evil one, and Burnt-Stick took the seat she was offered. Then the evil one went out of the lodge to climb his tree and wait for Burnt-Stick to come looking for him. After the man had been gone for a little while, Burnt-Stick held up her walking stick and said, "Walking stick, turn yourself into iron, and let that evil man impale himself upon you!"

The stick turned into iron, and so Burnt-Stick went to the tree where the evil man had hidden himself. Thinking that his plan had worked, the man leaped out of the tree at Burnt-Stick. But she held out the iron rod she had made out of the saskatoon walking stick, and the evil man was impaled upon it and died.

Burnt-Stick went back to the evil one's lodge. She healed all the women who had broken bodies, and she restored the dead ones to life. Selecting ten of the women to accompany her, Burnt-Stick finished her journey toward her brothers' house. When she arrived there, she found all her brothers in mourning. "Oh, oh, oh!" they cried. "The wendigo has eaten our little sister! The wendigo has eaten Burnt-Stick!"

Burnt-Stick stood before her brothers and said, "Do not mourn! I am here! The wendigo has not eaten me!"

The brothers rejoiced greatly that their sister was still alive. They listened in wonder as she told them her tale. Then she introduced the ten women she brought with her, "These women I saved from the evil one, and they have consented to be wives to you." Burnt-Stick's brothers married the women, and they were very happy together.

Not many days after the weddings, Burnt-Stick stood before her family and said, "I must leave you now. I am not a human being. I hear my father calling me back to him. I will turn into a deer, and in that form I shall leave you, since I have finished the work I was sent here to do."

The Double-Faced Ghost *(Cheyenne, Great Plains)*

A giant, two-faced supernatural creature also appears in this story from the Cheyenne people of the Great Plains. Unlike his wendigo counterpart, however, the Cheyenne ghost is not dangerous at all. He is generous, kind, and gracious, but most importantly, he is lonely and in want of a wife.

Once the ghost finds a woman he wants to marry, he goes out of his way to show the family that he is a good person. The family is, of course, quite frightened once they discover that a ghost has been helping them, but they treat the ghost with respect, and the father finds a way to honorably deny the ghost his daughter's hand without making the ghost lose face.

The game that the father plays with the ghost is called "hide-the-plum-pit" in the sources consulted for this book, but from the description of the game in the story, it would seem to be some version of the moccasin game, which was enjoyed by many Indigenous peoples, including Plains Indians such as the Cheyenne. The game uses three or four moccasins and a small object such as a pebble or a plum pit. One player hides the object under or inside one of the moccasins while using sleight of hand to disguise where the object is actually hidden, and the other player has to guess in which moccasin the object has been placed.

Once there was a ghost who was extremely tall. His legs were so long that he could cross a river in one stride or hop from hilltop to hilltop with no effort at all. His arms were long to match his legs, which made it very easy for him to catch any game he cared to hunt. But his height and his arms and his legs were not the oddest things about this ghost. No, his strangest feature was that his head had two faces, one facing front and the other looking behind, and so his name was Double-Face.

Double-Face liked that he could stride across rivers and over hills with great ease. He liked that he was a good hunter. And yet he was not happy because he had no wife, and of course being a ghost made it even more difficult for him to find a woman who might marry him.

One fine, sunny day, Double-Face decided to take a good long walk across the prairie. He strode along, feeling sad that he had no wife and wondering what he might do about his plight, when suddenly he saw a tipi off in the distance. The tipi was all by itself; there were no other tipis or people anywhere around it for miles. The ghost decided to go closer and see who lived in the tipi. Maybe there was even a woman who might consent to marry him!

The ghost crept as close to the tipi as he dared and then hid himself behind a convenient hill. He saw that three people lived in the tipi: a man, his wife, and their daughter. The ghost watched as the people went about their business, and as soon as he caught sight of the young woman, he knew he had found his bride. The young woman was so very beautiful, and the ghost could not wait to have her for his wife. But how to convince the family to let him marry her? It was unlikely that a living human girl would want a ghost for a husband, and her parents likely would not be happy with a ghost for a son-in-law. The ghost thought and thought about what he might do to convince the family that he would make a good husband for the young woman, and then he had an idea: he was a very good hunter, so he would bring the family fresh meat every day and leave it at the door of their tipi. Once they realized that he meant them no harm and would be a good provider, surely they would let him marry the young woman!

Pleased with his plan, the ghost set about to hunting, and soon he had caught a great deal of game. He dressed it, and just before daybreak, he left it on a clean antelope skin just outside the tipi. Then the ghost went and hid behind the hill to see what the people would do. When the sun came up, the people came out of the tipi and saw the great pile of meat the ghost had left. They were very happy to see that someone had given them this gift, but they were also puzzled. They looked around and called out their thanks to whoever had left them the meat, but when they saw no one and no one answered, they set about cooking and eating some of the meat and preserving the rest of it for another time.

This went on for several days. The ghost would go hunting and catch a lot of fat game, and then leave it in front of the tipi just before daybreak. Then the people would come out and try to find their benefactor, but since the ghost stayed well hidden, they never understood who would be so kind and generous to them.

Finally, the father had had enough of the mystery. "I am going to find out who it is that leaves us this fine game every morning," he said. "We really need to thank them, and I am tired of the mystery."

The father went a little way away from the tipi and dug a hole just large enough for him to hide in. Once it was dark, he got in the hole and waited. For a long time, nothing happened, and it was hard for him to stay awake. But just before dawn, the father saw something coming toward the tipi. It was incredibly tall and was carrying a bundle of game in its enormously long arms. Once the creature got close to the tipi, it left the game outside the door and strode away. That was when the father realized that the thing not only was a giant, but it also had two faces!

Once he thought it safe to do so, the father climbed out of the hole and ran into the tipi. "Wake up! Wake up!" he shouted to his wife and daughter. "Wake up! We must pack up our things and leave! I saw who has been leaving the meat. It's a huge ghost or monster or something, taller than the tallest tree, and it has two faces, one in front and one behind! We mustn't stay here a moment longer!"

The family hurriedly struck the tipi and packed up their belongings. They walked and walked all day, not daring to stop except to drink a little water and eat a little food. They wanted to get as far away from the monster as they could.

Sometime after the family had departed, Double-Face came back to the place where the tipi had stood to see whether the family had accepted his latest gift. There he found the meat lying on the antelope skin, but the tipi was gone. Double-Face looked at the ground and saw the family's tracks. He followed the tracks, and with long strides of his long legs, he caught up to them in no time. He stepped in front of them and said, "Wait! Please don't run away! I'm not going to hurt you! Won't you please listen to me?"

The family realized they had no way of escaping a monster who could cross a river in one stride or hop from hilltop to hilltop, so they stopped. The father said, "We are grateful for all the meat you left for us. We will listen to you. Tell us what it is you want."

"One day as I was striding across the prairie, I was feeling sorry for myself because I don't have a wife. Then I saw your tipi, and I saw your beautiful daughter, and I fell in love with her. I left you the meat because I want her to be my wife, and I wanted to show you how well I could provide for a family."

This certainly was a problem. The father realized that even if he thought it was good for his daughter to marry a ghost, it was unlikely that she would consent to marry one. The father thought quickly, trying to find a way to get his family out of this predicament without angering a large, strong, monstrous ghost who could easily kill them all if he decided to.

"Yes," said the father, "you have certainly shown that you will be an excellent provider, and I'm sure you'll make someone a fine husband someday. But there is a tradition among my people, a sort of challenge that suitors must conquer before he can marry one of our daughters."

"Oh?" said the ghost. "What challenge is that?"

"It's a little game called hide-the-plum-pit. We have to play it in order to see whether you are worthy to marry my daughter. If you win, you can marry her. If I win, you need to give something to our family."

"Hmm," said the ghost. "I have never heard of such a challenge or such a tradition. Are you sure we have to do this?"

"Oh, yes," said the father. "We must. This has always been the way of our people, and if we don't play the game first, then our family will be cursed."

"I would never want to be the cause of anyone being cursed," said the ghost. "I agree to your terms. What is it you would like me to give to your family if I lose?"

"Please continue bringing us fresh meat. You're such a good hunter, and we have been so grateful for your help."

"Very well," said the ghost. "Let's play the game."

The father brought out the plum pit, and they began to play the game. Now, the father had suggested this challenge because he knew no one could ever beat him at this game, even if it were a ghost from the land of the dead. The father's hands moved so fast that the ghost couldn't possibly find the plum pit, no matter how hard or how many times he tried. And of course it didn't help that the daughter had taken out her drum and had begun to play it and sing songs, which distracted the ghost no end.

Finally, the ghost gave up. "You win. I can't possibly defeat you. I'm very sorry that I won't be able to marry your daughter, but I will keep my end of the bargain."

"You are very gracious," said the father. "I hope you do find someone to marry soon."

And so the ghost continued bringing the family meat for the rest of their lives, but no one knows whether he ever found himself a wife.

The First Fog *(Inuit, Arctic)*

Sometimes creative acts happen out of the destruction of something evil, as in this Inuit story of how fog came into the world. A bad spirit has been graverobbing and then eating the bodies, and does not stop until the village angakkuq *deals with him. An* angakkuq *is a person who holds a special place in Inuit culture as a spiritual leader, peacekeeper, and shaman. This role may be filled by either men or women, but it is more common for men to become an* angakkuq.

In this story, we see the importance of the angakkuq *to the safety of his people and his role as someone able to deal with supernatural threats. When the people are troubled by the disturbance of their loved ones' graves by a bad spirit, it is the* angakkuq *who puts himself in jeopardy in order to discover why the graverobbing has been happening and to dispatch any supernatural beings who might be responsible. The* angakkuq *in this story also functions as a trickster, deceiving the bad spirit's wife about how to cross the river created by the* angakkuq's *magic, which results in the creation of the first fog.*

A long time ago, the people had a very dire problem. A bad spirit was coming down out of the mountains and stealing the bodies of the dead from their graves. No one knew who the spirit was or where it lived, and it was frightening to think that the spirit could come and steal a loved one's body any time it wished.

Finally the village *angakkuq* had had enough. He asked his fellow villagers to have a funeral and bury him as though he were dead. "I will wait in the grave for this spirit to come and get me," said the *angakkuq*, "and when it does, I will find out how to make it leave our loved ones' bodies in peace."

At first, the villagers were hesitant. "What if you die for real before the spirit comes to get you? What if the spirit kills you and eats you? What will we do then, if you are no longer here to help us?"

But the *angakkuq* reassured all the villagers that this was the best way to stop the spirit, and so they had a funeral for him and buried him in a grave as though he were dead. That night, after all the people had gone to their homes, the spirit came down out of the mountains to see whether any new bodies had been buried that day. He looked in the graveyard and saw the place where the *angakkuq* had just been buried. The spirit dug up the *angakkuq* and slung his body over his shoulders. Then he walked all the long way back to his house in the mountains.

When the spirit got home, he put the *angakkuq* down and said to his wife, "This one was heavier than all the others. I am very tired. I am going to sleep for a while."

"Very well," said the spirit's wife. "I will go out and gather firewood so that we can cook and eat this one later."

After the spirit's wife had gone, the *angakkuq* opened his eyes. The spirit's children had been watching him and saw him do this.

"Father! Father! This one isn't dead!" they cried.

"Hush," said the spirit. "I dug him out of the grave just this very night. He's dead for sure. Now let me sleep."

When the spirit rolled over to go back to sleep, the *angakkuq* jumped up and killed both the spirit and the spirit's children with his knife. Then the *angakkuq* ran out of the spirit's house and down the path that would take him back to his own village. As he ran, the *angakkuq* passed the spirit's wife as she was returning home with a load of firewood. At first, the spirit's wife thought that the *angakkuq* was her husband. "Where are you going in such a hurry?" she said as the *angakkuq* sped past.

Still thinking she had seen her husband running, and wondering what he was up to, the spirit's wife ran after the *angakkuq*. The *angakkuq* heard the footsteps of the spirit's wife following him. Soon the *angakkuq* reached a stream. He leapt over it easily. Then he turned and said to the stream, "Swell with water, little stream! Overflow your banks!"

By the time the spirit's wife arrived, the stream had turned into a wide river. It was so wide, the spirit's wife could not jump across it. She saw the *angakkuq* on the other side and shouted, "How did you get across this river?"

"Oh, it was very easy," said the *angakkuq*. "I just drank up all the water until the streambed was dry."

The spirit's wife knelt on the bank and began to drink. She drank and drank and drank until the streambed was completely dry. Then she started walking across. When she was in the middle of the streambed, the *angakkuq* said, "What is that dangling down from your private parts? Do spirits like you have tails like beasts do?"

The spirit's wife stopped and bent over to look. But because she was so full of water, her belly burst open when she bent over, and she died. The water that came out of her belly turned into fog, and this was the very first fog that ever existed. From then on, the people could bury their dead in peace, and no one disturbed the graves.

Coyote and the Origin of Death *(Caddo, Southeast))*

Coyote is a common figure in Indigenous myths, where he functions variously as a trickster, gullible mark, creator, or some mixture thereof. In this myth from the Caddo people of the southeastern United States, Coyote is responsible for death becoming permanent. However, he does this not through spite or by mistake but rather out of concern for the living, since if people do not die, there soon will be too many people, leading to a dearth of resources and much suffering. Despite Coyote's good intentions, the fact that he is the one who makes death a permanent state marks him as a pariah ever after.

In the beginning of the world, people never died. They just went on living and having children, and soon the world became too crowded and there was not enough food to go around. All the chiefs got together to hold a council to decide what to do.

One chief stood up and said, "I think we should have people die, but only for a little while. After they have been dead for a time, let them come back."

When that chief was done speaking, Coyote stood up and said, "Oh, no. That is a terrible plan. If people come back after a little while, we will still have the same problem because no one will ever go away forever. I think death should be something that is for always."

The other chiefs were dismayed by Coyote's words. "We should let people come back!" cried one.

"Yes!" cried another. "It's not fair that they should go away forever. Their families and friends will miss them so much if they know the dead will never return."

Many other chiefs also stood and spoke against Coyote's plan, and in the end, the council decided that people should die for a little while and then come back to life again. The medicine men then went about building a grass house facing to the east. This was a special house in which the dead were to be brought back to life.

"We will put an eagle feather over the door," said the chief medicine man, "and when somebody dies, the feather will fall off the door and turn red with blood. Then all the medicine men will know to come to the grass house and sing the spirit of the dead person back to life."

When the people heard the new rules about death, they agreed that this was a good plan. They did not want their friends and family members to be gone forever.

After a time, the feather over the grass house grew red with blood and fell off the door. The medicine men all went into the grass house, and for about ten days they sang to bring the spirit back to life. When they were done singing, the young man who had died was standing there in the middle of the grass house, alive again. Everyone who had known the young man rejoiced that he was alive among them once more.

Coyote saw what the medicine men had done. He saw the young man brought back to life and how the people rejoiced to see him again. But Coyote was not pleased. He wanted death to be forever because otherwise there wouldn't be enough food for everyone.

The next time the feather fell from the door, Coyote went into the grass house with the medicine men. Coyote sat there while they sang to bring the spirit back. After they had sung for many days, Coyote heard the sound of a whirlwind approaching the grass house. He heard the wind start to whirl and whirl around the house as the medicine men sang. Coyote knew that the spirit of the dead person was in this wind, and so when the wind approached the door of the house and tried to enter, Coyote jumped up and slammed the door shut, keeping the spirit outside. When the spirit saw that the door of the grass house was shut, it moved on with the whirlwind and never came back.

Because Coyote closed the door to the grass house that way, the spirits of the dead are never able to return to the land of the living. And when the people hear and see a whirlwind, they say, "Oh, that must be the spirit of someone who has just died. They are wandering and looking for a way to go to the land of the spirits."

Coyote, for his part, was frightened by what he had done, and so he ran away. And ever since that time, he has been very cautious because he always fears that he will be punished for making death last forever, and he is always very hungry for no one will give him food anymore.

Blue Jay and the Ghosts *(Chinook, Northwest Coast)*

Blue Jay is a trickster figure in the mythology of the Chinook people of the Pacific Northwest. Like many tricksters, Blue Jay is vain and selfish, and he likes to purposely go against the advice of others, especially that of his sister, Io'i. Blue Jay dismisses his sister's wisdom very frequently, often with the untrue observation that "Io'i always tells lies."

This story, which is primarily set in the world of the afterlife, both explains how ghosts continue their existence in the ghost world and also describes what that world is like, both for the ghosts who live there and for the living who might chance to visit them. The importance of politeness and respect, even to the ghosts of the dead, is a primary theme of this story, as is the importance of following directions given by a knowledgeable person, things that Blue Jay learns the hard way and at permanent cost to himself.

There was a time when some ghosts decided they needed a woman to be a wife for their chief. They looked among the living for the woman who would best suit. When they found her, they went to her family bearing a great wealth of dentalia shells, and her family agreed to the marriage. Io'i was married to the ghosts that night, but when everyone rose in the morning, they found that she had disappeared. Io'i's brother, Blue Jay, said, "I'll wait for a year, and if she has not reappeared or sent us a message, I'll go and look for her."

A year passed with no word from Io'i, so Blue Jay set out to find her. First he went and asked all the trees, "Where do people go when they die?" But the trees didn't answer him, so then Blue Jay asked all the birds. They didn't answer him either. Finally, Blue Jay asked an old wedge that belonged to him. "I know where people go when they die," said the wedge, "but I won't take you there unless you pay me." Blue Jay paid the wedge, and it took him to the land of the ghosts.

In the land of the ghosts, there was a large village with many houses. Blue Jay walked through the village, noticing that none of the houses had smoke rising from them, except for one very large house at the other end. Blue Jay went to the large house and entered. Inside he found his sister. They were very happy to see one another again, and after they had exchanged greetings, Io'i asked, "Why are you here? Are you dead now?"

"No, I'm not dead at all," said Blue Jay. "I paid my old wedge to carry me here."

Then Blue Jay went out of the big house and wandered through the village. He looked into each and every house, and found that all of them were full of bones. He returned to the big house, where he saw a pile of bones near where his sister was sitting.

"Why are all these bones in your house?" said Blue Jay.

Io'i pointed to one skull and said, "That's your brother-in-law."

Blue Jay thought, "That can't possibly be my brother-in-law. Io'i lies all the time."

But after sunset, when it was dark, the bones turned into the shapes of people, who began to go about their business. Blue Jay looked at them closely, but he found it difficult to see their features and their clothing.

"Where did all these people come from?" Blue Jay asked Io'i. "Where did all the bones go?"

"Don't be silly," said Io'i. "These aren't people. They're ghosts."

Blue Jay thought this a little frightening, but he said, "That's all right. I'd like to stay with you all the same."

"Very well," said Io'i. "How about going fishing? You can take your dip net and go out with that boy over there. He is a relative of my husband. But don't talk to him while you're out fishing together."

Blue Jay was unsure how he would talk to the boy, even assuming he found something to say. The ghosts only whispered, and no matter how hard Blue Jay tried, he couldn't understand what they said.

The ghost boy and Blue Jay went down to the river and launched their canoe, the ghost boy in the stern and Blue Jay in the bow. They paddled along for a while, and soon they came across a large group that was also paddling down the river. All the other people were singing as they paddled. Blue Jay recognized the song and joined in, but as soon as he started singing loudly, everyone else stopped. Blue Jay turned around to look at the ghost boy but saw that he had turned into a pile of bones.

For a while, Blue Jay continued to paddle along the river, neither speaking nor singing. Then he decided to turn around and see what had become of the ghost boy. When he looked, he saw that the bones had disappeared, and the ghost boy was sitting in the stern just as he had done when they started out.

Speaking very softly, Blue Jay asked the boy, "How far is it to your weir?"

"A little farther down the river," said the boy.

They paddled on for a short time. Then in a very loud voice Blue Jay asked, "How far is it to your weir?" When Blue Jay turned around, he found that the boy had turned into a pile of bones again.

Blue Jay remained silent for a few moments, then turned around and saw the boy sitting there. Blue Jay asked very softly, "How far is it to your weir?"

"It's right here," said the boy.

Blue Jay took his dip net and started to fish with it. He put the net in the water and brought up two branches, which he threw back in. Again Blue Jay dipped his net, this time bringing up a load of wet leaves. Blue Jay threw these back, too, but some of them landed in the bottom of the canoe, where the boy scooped them up.

They fished for a little longer, but all Blue Jay managed to catch were two more branches. "Oh, well," thought Blue Jay, "we may not be able to eat these, but they're still useful. I'll give them to Io'i to use on the fire."

The boy and Blue Jay paddled back home. It was very frustrating to Blue Jay to return with only two branches to show for all their work, but when they beached the canoe and headed back to the big house, Blue Jay noticed the boy carrying a mat full of trout. "That's odd," thought Blue Jay. "He never caught anything the whole time we were fishing."

The boy gave the fish to his people to cook. "Why do you have so few fish?" they asked.

"Blue Jay threw out almost everything he caught," said the boy. "It was so wasteful. He caught many fine, large fish, but then he just tossed them back into the water."

Io'i asked Blue Jay, "Why did you throw all the fish away?

"Fish?" said Blue Jay. "I didn't catch a single one. All I caught were a bunch of branches and a net full of leaves."

"Well, exactly," said Io'i. "You threw away a lot of good fish. The leaves were trout, and the branches were salmon."

Io'i left the house and went down to the riverbank. She looked inside the boy's canoe, and inside she found two very large salmon. She picked them up and brought them back to the house.

When Blue Jay saw his sister carrying the salmon, he was very surprised. "Where on earth did you get those?" he asked. "Did you steal them from somewhere?"

"Don't be silly," said Io'i. "You caught these. They were in your canoe."

But Blue Jay didn't believe his sister. "Io'i always lies," he thought to himself.

In the morning, Blue Jay went down to the riverside. He looked at all the canoes that had been beached there. Blue Jay wondered how he and the boy had been able to paddle out and not sink, since every single one of the canoes had holes in it, and in places they were dotted with moss and lichens.

Blue Jay returned to the house. "Your husband doesn't take very good care of his canoes," he said.

"Please stop complaining," said Io'i. "You're going to offend my husband and his family."

"But all the canoes are full of holes and have moss growing on them!"

"Well, of course they do!" said Io'i. "Don't you understand? These aren't living people here. They're all dead. They're all ghosts. They don't do things the same way you do in the land of the living."

After sunset, Blue Jay and the ghost boy went fishing again. This time Blue Jay teased the boy by shouting at him to turn him into bones, then being quiet until he became a boy again. Soon they arrived at the weir and began to fish. Every time Blue Jay caught some leaves or branches, he put them in the bottom of the canoe instead of throwing them away. When the canoe was full, they paddled back, and on the way home Blue Jay teased every ghost they met by shouting at them and turning them into bones. The boy and Blue Jay arrived back at the village. They beached their canoe and brought their catch into the big house.

"Look what we caught today!" Blue Jay announced as he gave his sister a great pile of big, fat salmon.

The next evening, Blue Jay went for a walk through the ghost village. When it was fully dark, all the bones turned into people and began to go about their business. As he walked, Blue Jay heard someone call out, "Look! There's a whale on the beach!"

Blue Jay headed back to the big house to find out more. His sister met him on his way. She pressed a knife into his hands and said, "Go and help carve up that whale!"

But Blue Jay didn't know exactly where the whale was. He went to the first ghost he saw and said very loudly, "Where is the whale?" but the ghost couldn't answer because it had turned all to bones. Frustrated, Blue Jay kicked the skull.

Blue Jay went on his way, asking every ghost about the whale, but he kept asking in a loud voice, and the ghosts kept turning into bones. Finally Blue Jay came across a large tree trunk at the edge of the river. The tree trunk had very thick bark, which the ghost people were stripping off with their knives. Blue Jay shouted at them, and the people all turned to bones. Then Blue Jay went up to the tree trunk and began peeling off some of the bark. He found that it was full of pitch. When he had peeled two big pieces, he picked them up and brought them home.

Blue Jay dumped the bark pieces just outside the house, then brought his sister out to show her. "Look at this!" said Blue Jay. "Everyone kept saying it was a whale, but it's nothing but a big tree with thick bark!"

"What are you talking about?" said Io'i. "That's whale meat right there. And it's good whale meat, too. Look at all the blubber!"

Blue Jay looked down, and sure enough, instead of two big pieces of bark, there were two big pieces of whale meat. When he looked up, Blue Jay saw another ghost coming toward the big house carrying a big piece of tree bark. Blue Jay shouted at the ghost, and it collapsed into a heap of bones. Blue Jay picked up the piece of tree bark and brought it back to the house. Then he went back out and did this over and over again, collecting all the whale meat that the ghosts were bringing home.

In the morning, Blue Jay thought that he would have some fun with the skeletons in the village. He went into a house where there were bones from a child and an adult. He picked up the skulls and put the child's skull on the adult's skeleton. Then he put the adult skull on the child's skeleton. Going from house to house, he switched up all the skulls that were there. When it got dark, the ghosts were in terrible distress! No one had the correct head. The children could not sit up properly because their heads were too big for their bodies. The adults all felt strange because their heads were too small for their bodies.

The next morning, Blue Jay put the skulls back on the proper bodies. Then he decided to play the same kind of trick, except with the legs. He gave the children's legs to the adults, and the adults' legs to the children. If there weren't enough children's bones, he'd swap a man's legs for a woman's, or the other way around.

Blue Jay thought himself a very clever fellow, but the ghosts soon became tired of all of his tricks. Io'i's husband said to her, "It's time your brother went home. He's behaving very rudely, and the people don't like him at all."

Io'i asked Blue Jay to stop behaving so badly, but he wouldn't listen. He kept doing things to the ghost people's skeletons in the daytime, and teasing them by shouting at them and turning them back into bones at night.

One day, Blue Jay went into the big house, where he found his sister cradling the skull of her husband. Blue Jay snatched it out of her hands and tossed it away. "Oh, no!" cried Io'i. "You have broken your brother-in-law's neck!"

When night fell, Io'i's husband was gravely ill. A shaman came to the big house and was able to heal him.

At last Blue Jay decided he should go home. Io'i handed him five buckets of water. "Now, listen carefully!" she said. "You will have to pass through five prairies and five woodlands on your way home. The prairies will all be on fire, but you must save all your water until you get to the fourth prairie. Don't forget what I just told you."

"I won't," said Blue Jay.

Blue Jay headed out with his five buckets of water. He walked until he came to a prairie. It was very hot there, and the prairie was dotted with red flowers. "This is probably what Io'i meant," said Blue Jay, and he poured out half of his first bucket onto the prairie, dripping the water onto the trail as he walked along.

Then Blue Jay walked on, and at the end of that first prairie he came to a woodland. He walked through the woodland and came to a second prairie. This one was on fire at the edge. He poured out the second half of his bucket onto that fire, and half of the next bucket as well. When he reached the end of the second prairie, he came to another woodland, and having crossed that, he came to the third prairie. Instead of just being hot or just being on fire on the edge, half of this prairie was ablaze. He poured one and a half buckets onto that fire and reached the woodland on the other side in safety.

Blue Jay came to a fourth prairie. This time, almost the whole thing was on fire, and Blue Jay only had two and a half buckets of water left. He poured out the half bucket that was left and then another half from one of the full buckets, and reached the woodlands in safety.

Finally Blue Jay came to the fifth prairie. This one was entirely on fire, and Blue Jay had only one bucket of water left. He poured out the whole thing as he walked along, and when he got to the end of his water he still had a little way to go to get to the woodland. Blue Jay took his bearskin blanket and tried to use it to beat out the flames, but the blanket caught fire and burned right up. Then the fire began to burn Blue Jay's hair, and soon he was dead, having been burnt to death by the prairie fire.

Around sunset, Blue Jay headed back to his sister's house. When he arrived on the bank of the river opposite from where she lived, he called out to her. Io'i came to the river and saw her brother's ghost standing on the other side.

"Oh, no!" cried Io'i. "My brother is truly dead."

Io'i took her husband's canoe and paddled it across to get her brother. When she arrived, Blue Jay said, "Where did you get this beautiful canoe? I've never seen one better."

"This is my husband's canoe, the one you said was all full of holes and covered in moss."

Blue Jay said, "Io'i, you always lie. Maybe this is your husband's canoe, but I know the other ones were all full of holes and had moss all over them."

"Blue Jay, you're dead now," said Io'i. "Things will look different to you here because now you're a ghost."

Soon they arrived at the village of the ghosts. Blue Jay and Io'i beached the canoe and headed back to the big house. Blue Jay saw all the ghosts going about their business. Some of them were playing games. Others were singing. Still others were dancing. Blue Jay tried to join in the singing, but all the ghosts laughed at him.

Io'i brought her brother into the big house. There Blue Jay saw a very handsome man, who obviously was a chief.

"Who is that?" said Blue Jay to his sister.

"Don't be silly," said Io'i. "That's my husband, your brother-in-law. You broke his neck once, remember?"

"And all those canoes on the riverbank," said Blue Jay, "they were just as beautiful as the one belonging to your husband. Not one of them had any holes or even one speck of moss."

"Oh, Blue Jay," said Io'i, "don't you understand? You're dead now, so you see the land of the ghosts the same way they do."

But Blue Jay didn't want to believe his sister. "Io'i lies all the time," he thought to himself.

Blue Jay decided to try one of his old tricks. He went up to a group of people and shouted at them, but instead of turning into piles of bones, they just laughed at him. When Blue Jay saw this trick wasn't working, he stopped trying.

Later, Blue Jay went for a walk again and found a group of magicians who were singing and dancing.

"Please share your powers with me!" said Blue Jay, but the magicians only laughed at him.

After a little while, Io'i came looking for her brother and found him watching the magicians and asking them for their powers.

"Don't be silly," Io'i said to Blue Jay. "Come home, and leave these people alone."

Blue Jay went home with his sister, but the next night he went back to the place where the magicians did their dancing. Again he asked them to share their powers with him, and again the magicians just laughed at him. Night after night, Blue Jay went to the magicians and asked for their powers, and on the fifth night the magicians had

had enough. They sent Blue Jay walking back to the big house on his hands, his legs waving in the air.

Io'i saw her brother prancing about on his hands. She began to weep and mourn. "Oh, Blue Jay," she cried, "now I have seen you die a second time, for the magicians have taken your wits from you."

Part III: Trickster Tales

Coyote and Little Turtle *(Hopi, Southwest)*

This story from the Hopi people of Arizona shows Coyote in his guise as a gullible creature who can be tricked into just about anything. When Coyote tries to bully a small turtle into singing for him, the turtle makes Coyote's gullible nature work to his own advantage, tricking Coyote into throwing him into the water, which is just where the turtle wants to be.

Near the village of Orayvi, there is a spring called Leenangva. All around the spring grew rushes and cattails and other plants that liked the water, and among the plants lived a family of turtles. The turtles lived there very happily. They had plenty of water and plenty of food to eat.

But there came a time when the rain did not fall. After a while, the streams and ponds began to dry up, and soon Leenangva also became dry. All the plants withered and died. It was hard for the animals who lived near the spring to find food.

Mother Turtle gathered up all her children and said, "We can't stay here. There is not enough water. There is not enough food. We need to go someplace else. We will go back to Sakwavayu, the

Blue Lake, where we used to live. Maybe there is enough food and water there."

And so the turtles began to walk to Sakwavayu, where they used to live. Because it was so very dry, and because the day was so very bright, the sand was extremely hot. The smallest turtle had a hard time walking because the hot sand burned his feet. He became very tired and footsore, so he stopped to rest in the shade of a bush, thinking that he'd sit there until he had cooled off and then go follow his mother and brothers and sisters. It was nice and cool in the shade, and Little Turtle was so very, very tired. Soon he fell asleep. Mother Turtle did not even notice that he was missing. None of the other small turtles noticed that he was missing either.

Sometime later, Little Turtle woke up. "Oh, dear, oh dear!" he cried. "I fell asleep for I don't know how long, and now Mother Turtle and my brothers and sisters have gone on without me!"

Little Turtle began to weep because he was lonely and frightened. He came out from under the bush and saw the tracks his family had left, going in the direction of Ismo'wala. Little Turtle started following the tracks, weeping bitter tears the whole time, fearing that he would never see his family again. And still the sand was so very hot and hurt his feet so very much.

Now, Coyote lived in Ismo'wala, and he heard the sound of Little Turtle crying. He went to see who was making that sound, and found Little Turtle weeping and following the tracks his family had made. Little Turtle saw Coyote coming, so he flopped down on his stomach and pulled his head and all his legs into his shell. Coyote went up to Little Turtle and sniffed and snuffed around him. Then he took his paw and flipped Little Turtle over onto his back.

"Sing me that song you were singing," demanded Coyote.

"I wasn't singing. I was crying," said Little Turtle.

"A likely story," said Coyote. "Sing me that song."

"I already told you. I wasn't singing, I was crying," said Little Turtle. "I fell asleep under that bush, and my family went on without me. I was crying because I'm afraid I'll never see them again."

"Oh, come on and sing already," said Coyote. "We both know you were really singing. If you don't sing, I'll gobble you right up!"

"You go ahead and do that," said Little Turtle. "It wouldn't kill me anyway. I'd still be alive inside your belly."

"Well, then, if you won't sing, I'll take you up that mountain over there and push you down the side," said Coyote. "You'll slide and slide on the snow."

"That's all right with me," said Little Turtle. "Sliding on the snow sounds like fun!"

"Well, then, if you won't sing, I'll take you and roll you around and around in the sand here," said Coyote. "It's very hot, and I bet you won't like that at all."

"Hot sand doesn't bother me," said Little Turtle, "and rolling around in it sounds like fun."

Coyote began to feel frustrated. Nothing he could threaten Little Turtle with scared him at all. Then Coyote had an idea.

"If you won't sing me your song," said Coyote, "I'll take you down to the river and throw you right in!"

"Oh, no!" cried Little Turtle. "Please don't do that. Please do anything else you like to me, but don't throw me in the river!"

"Hah!" said Coyote. Then he picked up Little Turtle in his jaws and trotted down to the riverbank. The river had plenty of water in it, and it was running fast. Coyote threw Little Turtle into the water. As soon as he was in the river, Little Turtle stuck his head and legs out. He called to Coyote and said, "Thank you so much! The river is where I live. Thank you for throwing me in!"

Coyote could not believe his ears. He became very angry. "I will eat that Little Turtle if it's the last thing I do!" he said, and then he jumped into the water. Little Turtle saw him coming, and dove under the surface. Coyote tried to catch Little Turtle, but the river was so full and moving so fast that Coyote drowned.

When Little Turtle saw that Coyote couldn't follow him anymore, he came to the surface and began to swim along. He knew the river would take him to Sakwavayu. Little Turtle soon reached Sakwavayu, where he saw that his family had not yet arrived, so he crept under a bush to wait for them. Little Turtle waited and waited, until the sun had nearly set and the sand had cooled. Then he heard the sounds of his mother and brothers and sisters talking and laughing as they walked along. Little Turtle came out from under the bush and shouted "Surprise!" at his family.

"My goodness!" said Mother Turtle. "How did you get here so fast?"

"When we were walking, I stopped to rest under a bush. I fell asleep. When I woke up, I saw that you had gone on without me. I was crying because I was afraid I'd never see you again. I started following your tracks, but Coyote heard me crying. He thought I was singing. He said that if I didn't sing for him, he'd eat me. Then he said he'd make me slide down the mountain on the snow. Then he said he'd roll me around in the hot sand. When he said all those things, I told him I wasn't afraid. Then he said he'd throw me in the river. I pretended to be very afraid, so he picked me up in his jaws and threw me in the water. I thanked him for bringing me to my home, but this made him angry. He jumped into the river, saying he was going to eat me, but the water was too deep and too fast for him, and he drowned. When I knew it was safe, I swam along the river until I arrived here, where I waited for you."

"What a good thing that silly Coyote believes anything anyone tells him!" said Mother Turtle. "I am very glad you were able to trick him like that. Now, let's go down to the water and find something to eat."

The turtle family went down to the water, where they found many good things to eat. And they lived at Sakwavayu ever after.

Coyote and Fox *(Shuswap, Subarctic)*

If the Coyote of the Hopi story is impatient and gullible, the Coyote of this Shuswap story is vain and vengeful, although here he certainly has good reason to be angry at first. We also see an example of the way that animal characters in Indigenous tales are seen as people, doing human things like hunting with weapons, using fire, and making and wearing clothing.

This story functions both as a cautionary tale and as a just-so story. It is a cautionary tale in that it shows us the price paid by people who are vain and greedy, and a just-so story that explains why the fur of the silver fox is considered to be so valuable. However, it is only the vengeful Coyote who pays a price for his sins; Fox steals Coyote's food and is just as vain of his fine cloak as Coyote initially is of his, but Fox gets away with a full stomach and his fine cloak intact.

Coyote was always traveling about, and one time he became hungry as he walked along. He came upon a dwelling inhabited by rock rabbits. Coyote thought to himself, "Now those would make a tasty meal, for sure!" So Coyote killed all the rock rabbits and strung them together on a string. He put the string over his shoulder and went on his way, thinking that he'd travel for a bit longer before eating his catch.

The day was very clear and very hot. Soon Coyote was tired and so hungry he couldn't go any farther. He found a good shady pine tree and sat beneath it. To cook his rock rabbits, Coyote first made a big fire. When it was nice and hot, he put large stones in the fire.

While the stones were heating, Coyote dug a hole, and when the stones were hot enough, Coyote put the stones in the hole. Coyote put the rock rabbits on top of the hot stones and covered them well with leaves and the dirt he dug out of the hole. Then he lay down in the shade of the tree to take a nap while his meal was cooking.

Now, Fox was also out and about on his travels, and as he walked along he saw Coyote asleep in the shade of the tree. Fox also saw the earth oven that Coyote was using to cook his meal. "I wonder what is cooking in there?" thought Fox, because he had been traveling all day and was very hungry. "I'll just go and have a little peek. Coyote's asleep; he won't even notice me."

Fox went over to the oven and dug out the rock rabbits, which were perfectly cooked. Fox gulped down half of them and was about to take the next one when Coyote said, "I don't mind sharing; just leave ten of them for me." Coyote didn't even sit up or open his eyes, he was that lazy.

Fox ate even more of the rock rabbits. "Leave nine of them for me, will you?" said Coyote.

But Fox kept on eating and eating, even though Coyote kept asking him to leave some for his own meal. Soon there was only one rock rabbit left. "Oh, well," said Coyote, "how about you leave half of that one for me?"

Fox didn't listen. He swallowed every last bite, and then all the rock rabbits were gone. Fox knew that Coyote would be very angry with him, so he left as fast as he could. This wasn't very fast, though, because Fox was so stuffed with good rock rabbits that he couldn't move very well, and soon he could go no farther. He lay down in the shade of a tree and went to sleep.

When Coyote realized that Fox had left after eating all the rock rabbits, he was furious. "That Fox! He didn't even leave one morsel for me! I'll show him!"

Coyote followed Fox's trail. Soon he came upon the place where Fox was fast asleep under the thick boughs of the tree. Using his magic, Coyote made the tree fall over on top of Fox. "There!" said Coyote. "That'll teach him to steal all my food!"

But the branches of the tree were so thick that the trunk never touched Fox at all. Fox squirmed his way through the thick branches and scurried away. Coyote saw him leaving and followed after, angrier than ever. Soon Fox came to a thick meadow of rye grass. He went deep into the grass, curled up, and went to sleep. Coyote watched Fox go into the grass, and when he was sure Fox was asleep, he set fire to the meadow. Fox woke up when he heard the sound of the approaching flames. He set his own back fire, and so he was able to escape.

Fox went to a place that was thickly grown with reeds. He went into the reeds thinking that maybe he'd finally be able to finish his sleep. But when he entered the reedy place, a great many hares jumped up and started running away. Coyote was still on Fox's trail, and so he saw all the hares running away. "Oh, this is fortunate!" said Coyote. "Now I'll be able to have a meal at last!"

Coyote set about killing the hares. Fox peered out from among the reeds and saw that Coyote was busy, so Fox slunk away. Coyote caught sight of Fox when he was a good way away, but now that Coyote had a great many fat hares to eat, he was content. "Fine, you can leave," Coyote called to Fox.

Coyote continued his travels until he came to a place where there were a great many magpies. Coyote set snares for the birds. When he had caught enough birds, he skinned them and made himself a fine cloak out of the skins with the feathers still attached. "Why, look how handsome this cloak is!" Coyote said. "No one will look better than me." Then Coyote made a song about how beautiful his cloak was and how pleased he was with it.

Again Coyote resumed his journey. Soon he crossed paths with Fox again. This time, Fox was wearing his own fine cloak, but this one was made of silver fox skins and was adorned with golden eagle feathers. Coyote was instantly envious of Fox's cloak, so he said, "Hey, Fox! Would you like to trade cloaks with me?"

"Of course not!" said Fox. "Why would I trade a cloak of fox fur and eagle feathers for one that is only made from magpie skins?"

Coyote pretended to accept Fox's answer. He turned away as though he were going to leave, but then suddenly jumped at Fox and snatched away the fur cloak.

Coyote ran and ran, clutching the fur cloak. Soon he came to a lake. He took the magpie-skin robe and tore it into pieces, then threw the pieces into the water. He picked up the fur cloak and put it on. My, how well he looked in it, and how beautiful the feathers were!

"I am the most beautiful creature on earth," said Coyote. "The only thing that is missing is a little breeze. How the feathers would flutter and dance if there was but a breath of wind! That is the only thing that would make me look better than I already do."

Now, Fox had followed after Coyote, and when Coyote got to the edge of the lake, Fox hid himself and waited to see what Coyote would do. When Fox heard Coyote wish for a breeze, Fox used his magic to call up a strong wind. The wind blew the fox-fur cloak off Coyote's back and carried it back to Fox.

Coyote knew he'd never get that fur cloak back, so he began to look around for the pieces of his magpie-skin cloak. But the wind had blown away many of the pieces, and the bits that Coyote was able to find had lost all their feathers.

Fox wore that cloak ever after, and soon he turned into an ordinary fox. This is why foxes have lovely silver fur, and why their fur is the most valuable one of all.

How Beaver Stole Fire *(Nez Perce, Plateau)*

A great many cultures have stories telling how one animal or another stole fire and gave it to the people. Coyote often plays this role, as does the opossum or, as in this story from the Nez Perce of the Columbia River Plateau in the Pacific Northwest, the beaver. Rather than being a substance that is simply created by or used by powerful beings, in this myth, fire is conceptualized as an inherent property of certain trees. The trees guard their fire jealously, and it's not until Beaver makes his brave attempt that fire is distributed to other trees and thus made available to other creatures as well.

Not only does this story explain how fire came to be used, but it also is a just-so story about certain geographical features. In Beaver's escape from the angry trees after stealing fire from them, the course that he runs along either digs or changes the channel of the Grande Ronde River.

In the time before there were any people in the world, animals and birds and plants walked and talked together just like people do now. And in that time, the only ones with the secret of fire were the pine trees. They guarded this secret very jealously and wouldn't give it to any of the other creatures, even if those creatures might freeze to death without it.

One winter, it was so very cold that all the animals were afraid they would freeze to death. Only the pine trees were warm, because they had fire. The animals held a council to see how they might go about stealing some of the pine trees' fire. They came up with plan after plan, but none of them ever succeeded until finally Beaver made an attempt.

Beaver knew that the pine trees were about to hold a great council near the banks of the Grande Ronde River in Idaho. He knew that it was so cold that the trees likely would light a fire to warm themselves. And so Beaver hid himself in a place where he could watch the pine trees as they prepared for their council. First, the trees went into the river to bathe, and the water was so very, very

59

cold! Then the trees came out of the river, and they built a fire to warm themselves after having bathed. But even as they shivered while they warmed themselves, the trees were still very crafty; they posted guards to watch for any animals or birds that might try to steal their fire.

However, Beaver knew they would post guards, and so he hid himself in a good place before the guards were there, but after the fire had been lit. As Beaver expected, soon a live coal came rolling down from the trees' fire to the place where he was hiding. Beaver jumped out of his hiding place, grabbed the coal, and ran away as fast as he could. The trees saw Beaver running away with a piece of their fire, and they went after him in hot pursuit. Whenever the trees got too close, Beaver would dodge this way and that, and this is why the Grande Ronde River has places where it is straight and places where it is crooked and winding.

After a long chase, many of the trees got too tired to continue running after Beaver, so they planted themselves on the banks of the river where they were, making a forest so thick that even the best hunters had difficulty moving through it. A few of the trees kept running after Beaver, but eventually they got tired, too, and planted themselves where they stopped. This is why in some places along the river there is dense forest, while in other places there are only a few scattered trees.

One cedar tree stubbornly refused to give up the chase, and kept running after Beaver after nearly all the other trees had stopped and planted themselves. A handful of other trees came with the cedar. Finally the cedar realized that he would never catch Beaver. He looked about and saw a high hill not far off.

"I will go and climb that hill," said the cedar to the other trees who were with him, "and that way maybe we can see where Beaver goes, even if we can never catch him."

The other trees agreed this was a good plan, so the cedar climbed up to the top of the hill and planted himself there on the crown. He looked down and saw Beaver diving into Big Snake River at the place where the Grande Ronde empties into it. As the cedar watched, Beaver swam across the Big Snake. Then Beaver went to the willows that stood on the banks of the river and gave them some of the pine trees' fire. After that, Beaver ran along the banks of the river for a little way, then dove back in and gave some fire to the birches on the other side of the river. And this is why when people make fire, they use willow and birch wood, because they have the fire Beaver stole, fire that will come out of their wood when it is rubbed a certain way.

And the cedar who climbed the hill? He stands there still, all alone, looking out over the river and over the trees that got pieces of the pine trees' fire, and when people go by that place, they tell the story and point out the lone cedar who chased Beaver all the way to that very spot.

The Raven and the Marmot (Alaska Native)

Raven plays a similar role in Alaska Native folklore that Coyote does in the stories of more southerly cultures. Raven is a trickster and a creator, but his hubris often leads him to be tricked by other animals.

Here Raven's pride is hurt by insults thrown at him by a group of seabirds. He tries to patch up his wounded dignity by going after a marmot, but the marmot is a quick-thinking animal and soon devises a way to escape Raven's beak by flattering the bird about his dancing ability.

The connection between dance and ravens is important to many Alaskan and northern Pacific Coast peoples. Several tribes from those areas practice forms of the Raven Dance, wherein the dancers don large wooden raven masks and sometimes feathered capes representing the bird's wings.

Unfortunately, I was unable to determine which Alaskan culture produced this particular story, but in her collection of Alaskan folktales, author Katharine Judson says that it is from the Bering Strait.

It was a fine, sunny day, and Raven thought he might go see whether he could find anything to eat at the seashore. As he flew along over the beach, a group of seabirds saw him gliding past and began to make fun of him.

One seabird called out, "Look at that Raven! He thinks he's so great, but all he ever eats is dead things!"

"Yes," said another. "I think that's just disgusting."

Then the birds began to taunt Raven together. "Carrion-eater! Carrion-eater! All you eat is dead things, and your black feathers are ugly!"

Raven was very put out by what the seabirds said. He turned away from the sea and flew toward the mountains, muttering to himself all the way. When Raven arrived in the mountains, he landed, thinking to rest his wings but still fuming over the things the seabirds had said. Raven looked about him and saw a marmot hole in the ground. Raven went to see whether the marmot was at home, but before he could so much as stick his beak into the hole, a small voice behind him said, "Excuse me, but that's my home. I'd like to go in, please, but you're blocking the way."

Raven turned around, and there was the marmot, waiting patiently for Raven to move aside. "Why should I move?" said Raven. "In fact, I think that maybe I should just eat you right now. That'll show those nasty seabirds they're wrong."

Marmot was puzzled by Raven's reference to the seabirds, but he said nothing about it. Instead, he said, "Very well, you can eat me, but I was wondering whether you might do one very important thing for me first."

Raven always liked being told how important he was, so he said, "Tell me what that is, and I'll see."

"I've heard that you are the best dancer in the world. I think that I should very much like your dance to be the very last thing I ever see in this world. If I sing, will you dance?"

Raven was extremely flattered by this. "Certainly! Begin your song, and I will dance for you. You will die happy."

"Oh, thank you!" said Marmot, and then he began to sing:

Oh, Raven, how gracefully you dance!

Oh, Raven, how beautiful your black feathers!

How strong your black beak!

Oh, Raven, dance for me, dance for me!

While Marmot was singing, the Raven began to hop about, first on one leg, then on the other. To concentrate better on his gracefulness, Raven closed his eyes. Soon Raven had hopped away from Marmot's hole, and the little creature scurried down into his burrow as fast as he could. When Marmot was safe from Raven's beak, he faced the entrance to his burrow and laughed. "*Chik-kik-kik-kik-kik*! That was the most ridiculous thing I've ever seen! I almost couldn't sing because I was trying so hard not to laugh at you. And now you won't get to eat me, even though I am fat and juicy!"

Raven couldn't think of anything to say to Marmot, even though he was very, very angry, so he flew away.

Woodrat and Pine-nut-man *(Pomo, California)*

The Pomo people of California traditionally lived along the north-central coast of the state in what are now Mendocino and Sonoma Counties, with their territory extending as far inland as Clear Lake. Like other Indigenous groups, the Pomo have many trickster tales, some of which feature the ubiquitous Coyote.

However, the Pomo also have stories involving a different trickster animal: Woodrat.

In this story, Woodrat tricks a strange manlike creature called Pine-nut-man, resulting in Pine-nut-man's eventual death from being drained of all the pine nuts that fill his skin. The villagers in the Sacramento Valley where Pine-nut-man meets his demise don't know what pine nuts are, but when they discover that they are good to eat, they greedily fight over them. This legend therefore functions as a just-so story, as many trickster tales do, showing both the cleverness of Woodrat and explaining the introduction of pine nuts into the Pomo diet as an important staple food.

The story below is based on one collected from Pomo informants by anthropologist Samuel Barrett in the early 20ᵗʰ century.

One day, Woodrat was feeling hungry, so he went out to gather pine nuts. When he got to the pine tree, he saw that Pine-nut-man had arrived there before him and was already up in the tree gathering pine cones. A few pine cones had fallen to the ground and lay at the foot of the tree. Woodrat picked up one of the pine cones and started digging out the seeds and eating them.

"Hey, brother-in-law!" Woodrat called to Pine-nut-man. "These are some awfully good pine nuts we have right here."

Pine-nut-man didn't pay any attention to Woodrat. He just went on picking pine cones and putting them into his carrying sack. Soon Pine-nut-man had picked all the cones on that tree. He climbed down with his sack and went a little way away from the tree, where he sat down and began to take the pine nuts out of their cones.

Woodrat watched Pine-nut-man for a while, and then he said, "I guess you don't want me here. Do you know what folks do when they don't want me around? They dig a big hole and throw me into it. I can't annoy people when I'm at the bottom of a hole."

Pine-nut-man was eager to get rid of Woodrat. He didn't like Woodrat watching him or talking to him while he was at his work. So, Pine-nut-man got his digging stick and began to dig a hole. He kept digging and digging until the hole was so deep, he could fit the whole length of his body into it standing up. Pine-nut-man had been digging for such a long time, he began to wonder whether Woodrat was even still there.

"Hey, Woodrat!" he called. "I'm almost done with the hole. Are you still there?"

"Oh, yes, I'm still here," said Woodrat, "but I'm not sure the hole is quite deep enough yet. Keep digging, and don't ask me any more questions."

While Pine-nut-man kept digging, Woodrat collected some rotten wood. Then he laid out his rabbit-skin blanket on the ground. He put the wood onto the blanket, and also a bow, some arrows, and a spear. Then he wrapped all those things inside the blanket and tied it well with thongs. Woodrat spoke to the bundle. "Bundle," he said, "speak to Pine-nut-man as though you were me."

Then Woodrat put the bundle next to the lip of the hole and ran far away from that place. He ran and ran until he arrived in the Sacramento Valley. In the valley there was a sweat lodge, and Woodrat went inside.

While Woodrat was running away, Pine-nut-man was still digging the hole. Presently, the bundle said to him, "Hey, Pine-nut-man! The hole is deep enough. Come and throw me in. Surely I'll break my neck at the bottom, and I won't be able to bother you anymore."

Pine-nut-man climbed out of the hole. He picked up the rabbit-skin bundle, thinking that it was Woodrat. Then he threw the bundle down the hole. When the bundle struck the bottom, it burst open, and Pine-nut-man saw the wood and weapons that had been inside it.

"Well!" he said to himself. "That Woodrat is much cleverer than I gave him credit for. But I'm cleverer still. He may have fooled me once, but he'll never fool me again. I can even see through mountains, and I'm the best tracker in the world. I'll follow Woodrat's trail, and when I catch him, I'll pay him out for tricking me."

Pine-nut-man looked around, and soon he found Woodrat's trail. He began following it, running along the same track Woodrat had gone, toward the Sacramento Valley.

Back in the valley, Blue Jay was perched on top of the sweat lodge that Woodrat had gone inside. Blue Jay was the chief of the village, and he had made it his duty to look for enemies from time to time so that the villagers could protect themselves. In the distance, Blue Jay saw a man running toward the village very fast.

"Hey, Woodrat!" said Blue Jay. "There's a man running toward our village. He seems very angry. Would you happen to know who he is?"

"Oh, that would be Pine-nut-man," said Woodrat from inside the sweat lodge. "And yes, I expect he's quite angry. I played a very good trick on him earlier today. But I know how to deal with him. Make sure all the entrances to the sweat lodge are completely sealed up, except for one small hole right at the top. I'll take care of the rest."

The other creatures did as Woodrat said. They sealed up the sweat house very tightly and made a small hole at the very top.

Just as they finished that work, Pine-nut-man ran into the village. He saw the animals gathered near the sweat lodge and said, "I am looking for my brother-in-law. I love him very much and haven't seen him in a long time. Would you happen to know where he is?"

"I'm right here," said Woodrat. "I'm inside the sweat lodge."

Pine-nut-man walked all the way around the lodge, but since it had been completely sealed up, he saw no way in.

"How do I get in?" said Pine-nut-man.

"There's a little hole at the very top," said Woodrat. "That's the way in. That's how we do things here in this village."

Pine-nut-man climbed up to the top of the sweat lodge and began working his way into the small hole. It was a very tight fit, and he had to work very hard to move his body through the hole. When Pine-nut-man had managed to get the lower half of his body into the sweat lodge, Woodrat took a sharp stick and poked Pine-nut-man hard in the stomach. A trickle of pine nuts started coming out of the hole. Woodrat poked him again, and this time more pine nuts came out. Woodrat poked him over and over until a great stream of pine nuts came pouring out of Pine-nut-man's body and piling on the floor of the sweat lodge. Soon all that remained of Pine-nut-man was an empty skin with a head, hands, and feet attached to it. There wasn't even a skeleton, because Pine-nut-man's insides were made of nothing but pine nuts.

When what remained of Pine-nut-man fell all the way through the hole, Woodrat opened the sweat lodge, and the villagers came inside. The villagers picked up Pine-nut-man's remains and put them outside the lodge.

Blue Jay looked at the great mound of pine nuts that had fallen out of Pine-nut-man's body. "Whatever are these?" he asked. "I've never seen anything like them. Can we eat them? Has anyone ever seen these before?" But none of the villagers knew what the pine nuts were, so Blue Jay sent a messenger to the next village to see whether they had anyone who knew about pine nuts.

The messenger came back with Grey Squirrel. The villagers invited Grey Squirrel into the sweat lodge and offered him a seat. When Grey Squirrel was seated, Blue Jay said, "Welcome to our village. We asked you here because we need your help. We have this big mound of something here, and we don't know what it is. Maybe you can tell us whether these are good or not?"

"I've never seen those before either," said Grey Squirrel, "but I'll taste one and let you know whether they are good."

Grey Squirrel picked up a pine nut. He sniffed it, then nibbled a small bit off the end. His eyes grew very big. Then he ate the whole pine nut.

"Oh, yes, I do know what these are!" said Grey Squirrel. "My people eat them all the time. They're quite delicious; we think they're the best kind of food in the whole world!"

Then Grey Squirrel took the sack that he had brought with him and filled it with pine nuts to take home, but when the villagers realized that the pine nuts were good to eat, they each wanted to get as much for themselves as they could. They grabbed their own sacks and started stuffing them with pine nuts. Soon fights began to break out when some villagers thought that others had taken more than their fair share, and one person slashed at Grey Squirrel's sack so that all his pine nuts fell to the floor. Grey Squirrel didn't have another sack, and none of the villagers would lend him one of theirs, so he went home empty-handed.

Woodrat watched how the villagers behaved over the pine nuts. He became so disgusted that he left and went far away.

Part IV: Hero Tales

Manabozho Plays Lacrosse *(Menominee, Northeast Forest)*

Manabozho is a culture hero in Algonquin cultures in both the United States and Canada. He has many different powers, and functions as both a trickster and a creator, as many Indigenous culture heroes do. This story features the version of the hero held by the Menominee people of what is now northern Wisconsin.

The central event of this story is a big game of lacrosse organized by the sky spirits and the underground spirits. Each group of spirits puts together a team of creatures associated with their various realms and pits them in a cosmic match on a field that extends from Detroit to Chicago.

Played with a small ball and sticks having a net at one end, lacrosse is an Indigenous sport that has been played in the northern United States and in Canada for many centuries. Although modern regulation lacrosse is played by a relatively small number of players on a relatively small field, matches played by Indigenous peoples before the incursion of Europeans were between teams that could include hundreds of players on a field that was several miles long. For Indigenous peoples, lacrosse was and still is a sacred game and was an important expression both of tribal identity and of spiritual beliefs.

Manabozho was a very clever and powerful being. Some even say that he made the whole world. Manabozho had a son, whose name was Wolf. One winter's day, Wolf told his father that he was going out to hunt. Manabozho knew that Wolf liked to hunt in the estuary at Green Bay, which was frozen over at this time of year.

"Take care, my son," said Manabozho, "and stay off the ice at Green Bay. It is very dangerous."

Wolf went out to hunt. He followed the game all the way around the bay until he was on the opposite side from his home. Wolf was already tired from his long day of hunting, and the sun was beginning to set. Taking a shortcut across the ice was so very tempting! Wolf thought for a long moment about his father's warning, but then he decided to run across the ice. "I am the swiftest runner in the world," said Wolf. "Surely I'll be able to get to the other side without coming to any harm."

Wolf began to run across the ice. But when he was only about halfway across, the ice began to crack and shudder under him. It broke up into small pieces that whirled about in the current. The ice was very slippery, and Wolf could not keep his footing. He fell into the deep, freezing cold water, where he drowned.

When Manabozho found out that his son was dead, he grieved heavily. Day and night, he wept bitter tears for his son, and with each of his sobs, the earth shook. Even the spirits began to be afraid.

"Let's give him his son back," the underground spirits said. "Who knows what Manabozho might do if his son stays among the dead?"

And so it was that Wolf returned to his father. "Look, Father!" he said. "I am alive again!"

"It doesn't matter," said Manabozho. "I've already wept too much."

Manabozho took a long branch from the fire, its end still aflame, and gave it to Wolf. "Take this fire," said Manabozho, "and go into the west, as far as you can go. Light fires there. From now on, when people die, their spirits will go that way."

Even though the underground spirits had given Wolf back, Manabozho remained angry that his son had died, and he vowed to take revenge on the spirits for allowing that to happen. Manabozho waited and waited for the best opportunity, but for a long time nothing presented itself. Then one day Manabozho was walking along, and he heard someone whooping with joy. Manabozho went looking for whoever it was that was making the noise, and soon he came across a little fish called Nakuti, who had been whooping over and over again.

"Hey, Nakuti," said Manabozho, "what is going on that you are so happy? I heard you whooping from very far away."

"Oh, it's the very best thing," said Nakuti. "The great spirits above the sky have challenged the great spirits under the ground to a game of lacrosse, so we're all going to play lacrosse tomorrow! The fish and animals are going to play for the spirits below, and the birds and thunder-beings are going to play for the spirits above, and I can't wait!"

Manabozho thanked Nakuti for telling him about the game and then went his way, elated. This was it; this was the moment he had been waiting for. Manabozho would go to this lacrosse game, where all the spirits would be assembled, and there he would avenge his son's death.

The day before the lacrosse game, the underground spirits went looking for the best place from which to watch the game, one goal of which was in Detroit and the other in Chicago. The spirits came up out of the water and climbed up a mountain that overlooked the playing field. Satisfied that this was the best place, they went back to their homes. Manabozho saw their tracks going up the mountain and back down again. He climbed the mountain himself and realized what the underground spirits must have been doing. Manabozho turned himself into a pine tree that was all burnt on one side, and there on the mountaintop, he waited.

The next day at dawn, all the animals, fish, birds, and thunder-beings arrived at the playing field. Each team was making the most raucous noises they could, trying to frighten their opponents. When everyone had arrived, each creature took on a human form and took his place on the field. Once all the players were in place, they all fell silent until the ball was tossed into play. Then with a great roar from each side, the game began. Up and down the field they ran, each team fighting to get possession of the ball and hurl it through their opponent's goal.

At one point, one of the teams got the ball and surged toward the Chicago goal. The opposing team redoubled their efforts, and in the melee that ensued, everything was such a blur of lacrosse sticks, arms, legs, dust, and shouts that Manabozho could not see what was going on. In his excitement, he forgot that he was supposed to remain hidden as a tree, and turned himself back into a man, hoping that he would better be able to see the game.

The sudden appearance of Manabozho in their midst startled the underground spirits. Realizing that he had accidentally revealed himself, Manabozho took his bow and arrows and began shooting the spirits. The spirits scurried down the mountain and dove back into the lake, trying to evade Manabozho's arrows, but it was no use: whoever Manabozho aimed at was pierced by an arrow. The rush of so many spirits back into the waters caused great waves to form on the lake. The waves sped over the shore of the lake and onto the playing field.

Now, the lacrosse players had seen the underground spirits racing back to the lake, and had heard them shrieking "Manabozho! Manabozho!" as they fled. The players all returned to the center of the field to decide what was to be done. It was intolerable that someone would be so brash as to attack the underground spirits.

"How are we going to find and catch Manabozho?" said one player.

"We'll use the power of the water," said another.

"Yes! The water will be angry with him and will show us exactly where he has gone," said a third.

The other players agreed that this was a good plan, so they all waded into the lake. When everyone had entered the lake, the water rose up and rushed out of the lakebed, intent on catching Manabozho and punishing him for shooting at the underground spirits.

Manabozho, meanwhile, had stopped shooting at the spirits and had started running away, because he knew that the spirits and their allies would never let him go unpunished. He ran away from the lacrosse field as fast as he could, but soon he heard a rush of water behind him. He looked back and saw the waters of the lake flooding after him.

Manabozho was terrified. He redoubled his speed, but no matter how fast he ran, the waters still were catching up to him. Faster and faster Manabozho went, and closer and closer came the water. Finally Manabozho ran past a mountain. He changed course and ran up the mountainside, thinking that he'd be able to escape the water by climbing higher. But it was no use; the water climbed the sides of the mountain.

On the top of the mountain was a tall pine tree. Manabozho ran up to the tree and said, "Oh, Little Brother! The waters of the lake are chasing me and will drown me if they catch me. Can you help me?"

"Certainly," said the tree. "What do you want me to do?"

"Let me climb into your branches, and when the water rises enough to catch me, grow another length to get away from it."

"Very well," said the tree, "but I can only grow another four lengths."

Manabozho scampered up the tree, getting to the top branches just as the waters of the lake began swirling around the roots of the tree. But Manabozho was still not safe; the waters rose and rose until they were almost touching his feet.

"Little Brother!" said Manabozho to the tree, "please grow!"

And so the tree grew another length, raising Manabozho well above the flood. But this didn't last long, for the waters continued to rise quickly.

Again Manabozho asked the tree to grow, and again it grew and raised him above the flood. Still the waters rose around the tree trunk. A third time Manabozho asked the tree to grow, and the waters rose even more, threatening to reach Manabozho and drag him into the depths.

"Oh, Little Brother, please grow one last time!" said Manabozho to the tree.

The tree shot up its fourth and final length. There Manabozho closed his eyes, clung to the branches, and waited for death, but when he opened his eyes to see whether the waters were still rising, he found that they had stopped and that he was safe.

Glooscap and Uncle Turtle *(Wabanaki, Northeast Forest)*

Glooscap is the culture hero of the Wabanaki peoples from the northeastern United States and the Canadian Maritime provinces. The term "Wabanaki" does not refer to a single culture but rather to the confederacy of the Mi'kmaq, Maliseet, Passamaquoddy, Abenaki, and Penobscot peoples.

In this story, instead of fighting monsters or doing other brave deeds, Glooscap plays something of a secondary role to his old Uncle Turtle, an ugly, lazy old man. Uncle Turtle, who also is called Mikchich, acts as something of a foil to his handsome, strong young nephew. Glooscap uses his powers to turn Mikchich into a young and handsome man so that he can get a wife, but nothing Glooscap does for his uncle can change his lazy ways. Mikchich learns a hard lesson in humility and following instructions when he ends up trapped under the body of a whale that Glooscap gives him the strength to lift by himself.

There was a time when Glooscap went to Pictou to stay with his Uncle Turtle. Glooscap arrived in the village but would not stay as a guest with anyone but his old uncle. This was very disappointing for the young women of the village, for Glooscap was very strong and handsome, and they all wanted him to come and stay in their wigwams instead. "Why is that handsome young man Glooscap staying with Mikchich, that ugly old Turtle?" they complained. "It isn't fair that he should choose that lazy old man over beautiful young women like us."

But Glooscap did choose to stay with his uncle, for even though Mikchich was old and ugly and very lazy, Glooscap was fond of him and wished him well.

One day, Glooscap said to Mikchich, "Uncle, why have you never married? We should find you a wife. You shouldn't have to live here all alone."

"Bah," said Mikchich. "Who would have me, looking as I do? I may be old, but I'm not deaf, and I'm not blind. I know what the young women think about me. No, there's no point in looking, Nephew. No point at all."

"Maybe," said Glooscap, "but there is to be a great feast in the village in a few days' time. There will be many young women there. Perhaps you will find a wife at the feast."

Mikchich scoffed. "Even if I were as handsome as you, I still do not have the right clothes to wear to a feast. I'm poor, and my clothes are ragged. Everyone would still laugh at me. I'd rather stay home where I'm comfortable. You go to the feast, Nephew, and enjoy yourself. I'll just wait for you here."

Glooscap didn't really want to go to the feast himself, but he did want to help his uncle. So he said, "Uncle, what if I help you? What if I make you handsome and give you good clothes to wear? Would you go to the feast then and look for a wife?"

"If you can do that, then yes, I'd gladly go," said Mikchich, not believing that Glooscap could change him like that.

Glooscap took off his belt and handed it to his uncle. "Here, Uncle," he said, "put this on, and we'll see what follows."

Mikchich took Glooscap's belt and put it on. His skin began to smooth out and become a young man's skin. His skinny old limbs became rounded with muscle. His ugly face became very handsome. His ragged clothes changed into the finest anyone had ever seen. Soon there were two handsome young men standing in Uncle Turtle's wigwam.

"Well, look at me now!" said Mikchich. "I am certainly ready to go to the feast and to find a wife!"

Mikchich went to the feast. He entered the games and competed with all the young men. Every game he entered, he won, and all the young women were very interested indeed in this new stranger who was more handsome and stronger and more skilled than all the other young men there.

While the young women were watching Mikchich, he was watching them. He saw many beautiful women that he thought would make any man a fine wife, but his eyes kept coming back to one woman in particular. She was more beautiful than all the rest, and by the end of the day, Mikchich had his heart set on her. Mikchich went back to his wigwam and said, "Nephew, I have found the woman I want to marry. It is the youngest daughter of the chief."

"That is good!" said Glooscap. "I will go and ask her parents for you."

Glooscap took a bunch of wampum and went to the chief's wigwam. There he spoke to the young woman's parents and gave them the wampum.

"Should we let our daughter marry this Mikchich?" said the chief to his wife.

"Yes, I think he would make her a very good husband," said his wife. "I saw him at the feast, and he seems to be a fine man."

The chief called his youngest daughter to him. "We have found you a husband," he said. "Prepare a good meal, and fix up a couch for your young man."

The young woman did as her father said. She took good venison and cooked a meal, and while it was cooking, she made a couch out of the boughs of trees and covered it with a blanket of furs. When all was ready, the young woman went to Mikchich's wigwam to fetch him. The young woman brought her new husband back to her parents' wigwam, where he sat on the couch she had made and ate the meal she had prepared, and so Mikchich and the young woman were married.

Sometime after the wedding, the young woman went to Mikchich and said, "You need to go hunting. We don't have enough food. We are going to starve."

Mikchich was very lazy. He didn't want to go hunting. But his wife was insistent, so he left the wigwam, thinking that he would walk around for a while and then go home and tell his wife he hadn't been able to catch anything. During his walk, he went down by the seashore, where he found some of the men trying to pull a whale they had caught up to the village. "Aha!" thought Mikchich.

"I know how to make my wife think I am a good hunter and a good husband, and it will be easy."

Mikchich went to his nephew, Glooscap. He explained that he wanted to bring the whale home so that he could show his wife what a good provider he could be. Glooscap listened carefully to his uncle and then said, "All right. I'll give you the strength to move the whale all by yourself. But don't take it any farther than your father-in-law's wigwam!"

Mikchich went down to the beach, where the men were still struggling to pull the whale ashore. "I can help with that!" said Mikchich. "I'll take it up to the village myself."

The other men laughed. "If we can't even pull this great beast onto the beach when twenty of us are working, how do you think you'll fare carrying it by yourself?"

Mikchich insisted, so the men let him try, thinking that at the very least they would be able to laugh at Mikchich's efforts. They didn't laugh long, for Mikchich waded into the surf and put his shoulders under the whale. He gave one great heave and put the whale on his back. Then he started walking back to the village, carrying the whale all by himself, while the other men of the village stared in disbelief.

"This is easy!" said Mikchich. "Why should I stop at the chief's wigwam? I'll take this all the way to my own place, and my wife will see what a mighty hunter I am, and so will all the men! We'll see who's laughing when I'm done with this."

This was a big mistake. Because Mikchich was thinking about how wonderful he was and how everyone would be envious of him, and how he would do even more than Glooscap told him to do, Mikchich stumbled on his way into the village, and the whale came crashing down on top of him. The people all gathered round the whale, wondering what to do. Soon Glooscap arrived.

"Your uncle is underneath the whale!" cried the people. "He stumbled when he was carrying it, and now he is crushed flat! What should we do?"

Glooscap laughed. "My uncle will be fine," he said. "Just cut up the whale right here, and bring the pieces back to the village."

The villagers did what Glooscap said. They cut up the whale and brought it back to the village, where they prepared a great feast. When the food was all cooked and the people were all sitting and eating and enjoying themselves, who should wander into the village but Mikchich, looking none the worse for the wear!

Mikchich realized the people were staring at him. "Oh, don't mind me," he said, "I was just taking a nap on the beach."

And to this day, turtles have flat shells because of how Uncle Turtle was crushed by the whale.

Brave Woman *(Hunkpapa Sioux, Great Plains)*

Some Indigenous stories feature female heroes whose bravery and strength save their people from disaster or win honor for themselves and their families. The tale below, from the Hunkpapa Sioux, explains how a young woman named Brave Woman avenged the deaths of her brothers, who had been killed in battle against the Crow. Although this story is being presented in a book of myths, it is quite possible that it has a basis in historical fact.

Fighting over access to territory and food resources was common among the Plains Indians. In these battles, warriors could perform different kinds of brave acts to help their people win and also to garner personal glory for themselves. One such act was known as "counting coup," in which the warrior rode up to an enemy, touched him with a hand or a stick, and then rode away. Counting coup on an enemy gave the warrior great status, and it was considered to be an extreme disgrace to allow an enemy to count coup on oneself.

Brave Woman rides into battle not to fight and kill but to count coup, in order to bring disgrace on the warriors who killed her brothers. Although Brave Woman's father is saddened by her desire to ride into battle, he does not try to stop her. Instead, he grants her the honor of carrying his own coup stick and wearing his own eagle-feather war bonnet into the fray.

This story is based on a version told by Jenny Leading Cloud, a member of the Rosebud Reservation in South Dakota.

Long, long ago, before the white people came to what is now Minnesota, there lived a chief of the Hunkpapa Sioux named *Tawa Makoce*, or "His Country." He was a great warrior in his prime and a very wise leader. His people trusted and honored him. His Country had four children: three sons and one daughter. The daughter was called *Winyan Ohitika*, which means "Brave Woman."

Now, at that time, the Hunkpapa were often at war with the Crow tribe. The Hunkpapa and the Crow fought a great many battles, and when His Country's sons were old enough, they went to war, hoping to prove themselves and to live up to their great father's example. But His Country's sons did not share their father's good fortune. One by one, the three young men were killed in battles against the Crow, and soon of His Country's four children only Brave Woman was left.

Brave Woman was very beautiful. Many young men wanted to have her for a wife, but every time a young man's father went to ask her to be a bride for his son, Brave Woman refused. It did not matter how handsome the young man was or how many horses the young man's family offered as dowry. Brave Woman would not agree to marry any of them. To each one, she said, "All my brothers have fallen in battle against the Crow. I will not marry until I have gone out to battle myself to avenge their deaths."

There came a time when the Crow tried to take more territory along the Upper Missouri River, territory that the Hunkpapa considered to be their own. The Hunkpapa mounted a war party to go after the Crow and make them retreat from the area they had just taken. Among the war party were two young men who had vied for Brave Woman's hand. One was named Red Horn, and the other was Little Eagle. Red Horn was the son of a chief, and his father had tried many, many times to get Brave Woman to agree to marry his son. But Little Eagle was from a poor family, and even though he loved Brave Woman very much, he was never able to get up the courage to ask for her hand himself.

When Brave Woman saw that a war party was going out to confront the Crow, she saw that her time for vengeance had come. She put on her best clothing and took up her brothers' weapons. She readied her father's best horse. Then she went to her father and said, "Father, the time has come for me to go and count coup against the Crow. The time has come for me to avenge my brothers. Please don't try to stop me; this is something I must do."

"My daughter, you are my only remaining child. I wish you would stay home with me. But I know how strong is your desire, and it is a good desire. You may go, with my blessing. Here is my war bonnet. Wear it proudly. Do what you must do."

Brave Woman put on her father's war bonnet. She mounted her pony and went to join the war party. At first, the warriors were surprised to see her, but they did not ask her to leave. Brave Woman went to Red Horn. "Take my eldest brother's lance and shield," she said. "Count coup for him with them." Then she went to Little Eagle and said "Take my middle brother's bow and arrows. Count coup for him with them." Brave Woman gave her youngest brother's war club to another warrior. For herself, she kept her father's own coup stick.

The war party came across a Crow encampment and rode down to attack. Brave Woman did not go with the first charge; she stayed back and sang war songs and made the war cry that Sioux women make to encourage their men while they fight. Soon it became clear that the Hunkpapa were unlikely to succeed. They were greatly outnumbered by the Crow, and as the Crow pushed the Hunkpapa war party back, Brave Woman spurred her pony and rode into the fray. Brave Woman did not try to injure or kill the Crow warriors. Instead, she touched them with her father's coup stick, counting coup for her dead brothers. When the Hunkpapa warriors saw how courageously Brave Woman rode here and there among the Crow, they rallied, and for a while it seemed they might drive the enemy back.

But the press of Crow warriors was too great. The Hunkpapa were driven back again. Suddenly, Brave Woman's pony lurched and went down. He had been killed by a musket shot. Red Horn saw Brave Woman fall. He rode past her without so much as looking at her, and Brave Woman disdained to ask him for help. A moment later, Little Eagle galloped over to where Brave Woman was standing. He dismounted and asked her to get on his pony.

Brave Woman mounted the pony and waited for Little Eagle to join her. "You have to go alone," said Little Eagle. "My pony was wounded in the battle. He won't be able to carry both of us safely."

"I can't leave you here on foot!" said Brave Woman. "The Crow will surely kill you."

For answer, Little Eagle took Brave Woman's brother's bow and slapped the pony on the rump with it. The pony bolted and carried Brave Woman away from the battle. Little Eagle himself went back into the battle to help his war party.

When Brave Woman was able to get control of the pony, she went back to the battle as well. There she rallied all the Hunkpapa warriors, and they were so roused by her courage and fury that they beat back the Crow, despite their overwhelming numbers. The Crow had to admit defeat, and so they left the Upper Missouri.

The Hunkpapa were grateful for their victory, but they also mourned for all the warriors who had fallen in the battle. Among the fallen was Little Eagle, who had so bravely helped his friend. Red Horn was scorned for leaving Brave Woman to die. His bow was broken, and he was sent back to his own people.

The Hunkpapa took Little Eagle's body to the place where the Crow had been encamped. There they erected a scaffold high above the ground and placed Little Eagle upon it. They killed his pony underneath the scaffold so that he might continue to serve Little Eagle in the afterlife.

Back in the Hunkpapa camp, Brave Woman slashed her forearms and cut her hair. She tore her fine robe. She did all these things to show that she mourned for Little Eagle. For the rest of her life, she refused to marry anyone and asked that she be treated as though she were Little Eagle's widow. The people honored her request from that moment on.

Blood Clot Boy *(Ute, Great Basin)*

The buffalo was one of the most important sources of food, clothing, and shelter for the peoples of the Great Plains and the Great Basin in the western United States. It is no surprise, then, that the buffalo also figures largely in the storytelling of these cultures.

Blood Clot is a culture hero associated particularly with the buffalo, and is held in common by many tribes from the Plains and the Basin. In this story from the Ute people, Blood Clot has a miraculous birth from a clot of buffalo blood that is placed in a kettle to be made into soup for two elderly people who are starving. That Blood Clot is a supernatural being is confirmed by his prodigious growth; it only takes a few days for him to reach physical maturity, after which he shows supernatural prowess in hunting that it is dangerous for others to witness.

As is the way with such beings, Blood Clot does not spend much time among ordinary humans. When Blood Clot's wife breaks the taboo against saying the word "calf" in her husband's hearing, Blood Clot flees the encampment of the people and turns into a buffalo, in which shape he roams the prairies ever after.

A long time ago, there lived a very old man and his wife. Life was very difficult for them. The old man tried his best to hunt to bring back food, but they lived in a place where game was very scarce, and so they often went hungry.

One day the old man went out to hunt. As he walked along, he noticed a set of buffalo tracks. The old man's heart rose. If he could get just one buffalo, he and his wife would eat well for a long time! They could feast on fresh meat tonight and dry the rest for later.

The old man followed the tracks carefully, but the only thing he found was a large blood clot on the ground. He picked up the clot gently, folded it in his shirt, and went home, where he gave the clot to his wife to cook. The old woman put the blood clot in a pot with some water and set it over the fire, but when the pot began to steam, suddenly there were cries coming from inside the pot! The old man went to the pot and looked inside. Instead of the blood clot, there was a small baby boy, waving his fists and crying. The old man took the boy out of the pot. The old woman bathed him and wrapped him in warm clothes, and soon the baby had gone to sleep.

In the morning, the old couple was surprised to find that the baby had grown in the night. He continued to grow throughout the day. By sunset, he was big and strong enough to crawl about. The next day, he was trying to stand up, and the day after that, he began to walk by himself. The old couple named the boy "Blood Clot," and they raised him as their son.

Soon Blood Clot was big enough to go out hunting. His father made him a bow and arrows, and every day Blood Clot would hunt and return with something for the family to eat. Sometimes he caught a rabbit. Sometimes he caught a deer. Other times he brought home birds. But he never came home empty-handed, and the old couple rejoiced that they were never hungry anymore.

One day, when Blood Clot had grown into the stature of a young man, he went to his parents and said, "I would like to go and find another village and meet new people. I will not leave you hungry; I am going to go hunt now and will hunt all day and all night. You need to stay inside the tipi. Weight the edges down with rocks, and close the door securely so that the tipi won't blow away. No matter how the wind may howl, you must stay inside. I will call you when you can come out."

The old couple did what their son instructed. They spent the day inside the tipi, but all was quiet. At sunset, they went to sleep and slept soundly until daybreak when the sound of a loud wind began to rush all around their home.

"I must go and see what this whirlwind is," said the old man, but his wife said, "No! We must stay inside as Blood Clot told us to do."

The old man stayed inside, and he and his wife shivered in fear as the wind roared and roared around their home and shook the tipi. Suddenly, the wind stopped, and they heard Blood Clot calling to them. "Mother! Father! You can come outside now!" he said.

The old couple left the tipi and gaped in astonishment. All around their home were dozens of dead buffalo. "I have killed all of these for you," said Blood Clot. "You can dry the meat and cure the hides. This will last you a long, long time. Soon I must be on my way. Mother, will you pack a little food for me to take with me?"

"Yes, my son," said the old woman. She packed him some pemmican to take with him while he readied himself for the journey. When all was ready, Blood Clot said goodbye to his parents and set out to find a village with many new people for him to meet. He wore his best buckskin breeches and brought with him his best bow and a fine quiver of arrows.

After a few days, Blood Clot came across a village of people. He went to one of the people who lived at the edge of the camp and asked where he might find the chief. The man told Blood Clot that the chief's lodge was in the center of the camp. Blood Clot went to the lodge. There he found the chief and his daughter sitting together outside.

"Welcome," said the chief. "Sit down with us. Tell us your name and who your people are."

Blood Clot thanked the chief and sat down. "My name is Blood Clot, but I don't know who my people are. I am here to visit with you."

The chief invited the other villagers to come and meet their new visitor. Everyone came to the chief's lodge, even though they were weak with hunger from lack of game. When everyone was gathered, the chief said, "This young man is called Blood Clot. He says he doesn't know who his people are. Maybe one of us knows?"

"Are you from the Deer people?" asked one. Blood Clot said that he thought not.

"What about the Otter people?" asked another.

"No, that doesn't sound right either," said Blood Clot.

The people listed tribe after tribe, but none of them sounded right to Blood Clot until an old man said, "Maybe you are one of the Buffalo people. As I look at you here, I feel that you are of the Buffalo tribe."

Blood Clot thought about this for a moment, then agreed that this sounded right. The people of the village liked Blood Clot very much. They asked him to stay in their village, and soon they asked him whether he would like to marry the chief's daughter. Blood Clot agreed, and the young people were wed.

On the evening of the wedding, Blood Clot went to his father-in-law and said, "Please bring me one arrow from your tipi. Then tell all the people in the village to put rocks at the bottom of their tipis to hold them down, and to tie the doors shut securely. You should do the same with your tipi. Around daybreak, you will hear the noise of a great whirlwind, but you all must stay inside. I will let you know when it is safe to come out."

The chief and the villagers did as Blood Clot instructed, and at daybreak they heard the noise of a strong wind blowing through their camp. It shook the tipis, and the people were frightened, but they stayed inside until the wind stopped and they heard Blood Clot calling to them.

"Come outside!" said Blood Clot. "I have something good to show you!"

The people came out of their tipis and gasped in astonishment. At the door of every tipi in the village, there was a dead buffalo. The people dressed the buffalo and prepared some of the meat for a great feast. The rest they dried to use later, and they prepared the hide and bones and organs in their traditional ways to use for tools and clothing and other needful things.

At the feast, Blood Clot told his wife, "Because I am of the Buffalo people, you must never say the word 'calf' in my hearing. The Buffalo Calf is part of who I am, and you must not say that word."

Blood Clot lived happily with his wife in her village for a long time. But then one day a herd of buffalo was passing close to the village. Blood Clot and the other hunters went out and killed many fine buffalo. While the people of the village were skinning and dressing the dead animals, another herd of buffalo passed very close to the village. At the outer edge of the herd was a fine young calf. Blood Clot's wife saw it, and forgetting what her husband had told her, she shouted, "Kill that calf!"

As soon as Blood Clot heard his wife's shout, he jumped on his horse and rode toward the buffalo. Blood Clot's wife ran after him, crying and shouting for him to come back, but to no avail. As Blood Clot entered the herd, he began to change form, and soon he was a buffalo himself. Blood Clot never returned to his village. From that time on, he remained a buffalo and ran with his herd.

Part 2: Cherokee Mythology

Captivating Myths and Legends of a Native American Tribe

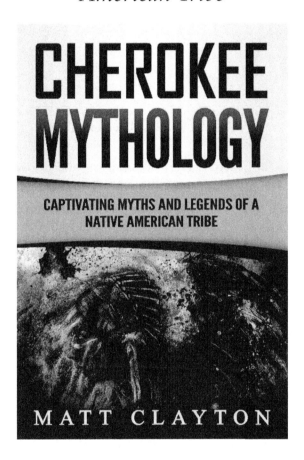

Introduction

The Cherokee are an Indigenous American tribe whose lands were originally in the southeastern part of what is now the United States. However, they appear to have settled there after migrating from lands further north. The Cherokee language is in the Iroquoian language family and has its own writing system: a syllabary developed in the early nineteenth century by Sequoyah, a Cherokee man, who worked as a blacksmith and silversmith. He wanted to create a means by which his people could read and write in their language.

The earliest contact between the Cherokee and Europeans appears to have been the 1540 arrival in Tennessee of Hernando de Soto. In 1567, another Spanish group attempted to settle in Cherokee lands but were rebuffed. Settlements by Scottish, Irish, and English colonists could not be dislodged, though, and the Cherokee began losing their native lands to white settlers, with devastating consequences to the tribe. The settlers brought diseases to which the Indigenous peoples had no immunity, and the deaths that ensued significantly diminished the Cherokee population. In 1835, the Cherokee were rounded up and forced to march from their homes in the Southeastern United States to the Oklahoma Territory, where they were put on reservations. The Trail of Tears was a major traumatic event for the Cherokee; not only did they lose their homes and their lands, but many people died from the hardships of the march, while others took their own lives rather than allow themselves to continue to live under the domination of white colonists.

In the twentieth century, the conversion of the Oklahoma Territory into the state of Oklahoma in 1907 led to a dismantling of much of the infrastructure the Cherokee had built to govern themselves and educate their children, including the loss of some reservation lands to a new generation of white settlers. It was not until the 1960s that the Cherokee began to regroup and reorganize themselves as a nation, which culminated with the ratification of a new tribal Constitution in 1975. Today, the Cherokee people continue to occupy reservation lands in Oklahoma, where they practice Indigenous foodways and medicine and engage in traditional pastimes such as stickball—a game similar to lacrosse.

In Cherokee myth—as in other Indigenous American traditions—the whole of creation is alive and able to communicate like humans and with the human beings who share their environment. Cherokee myths explain how the world came to be the way it is, and impart important lessons about Cherokee cultural values. In the brief collection of stories retold in this volume, you will learn why the opossum has no fur on its tail, how the bat and the flying fox were created, and how medicine and disease came to afflict human beings, while the misfortunes and desires of animals and birds become expressions of important Cherokee cultural values, such as modesty of speech, humility, and gratitude for the earth's bounty. Like the human beings with whom they share their world, the animals and birds play stickball and hold dances, and they have councils in townhouses—communal spaces that were an important part of Cherokee settlements.

These stories are very old—passed down from generation to generation by storytellers who wished to instruct, entertain, and keep their traditions alive. They are part of a living tradition; the cultural fabric of an Indigenous American people who have survived against terrible odds, continue to live according to their traditional values and wish to create a better future for themselves and their children.

Why the Possum's Tail is Bare

Everyone knows that the opossum has a bare tail today—it is long, pink, and hairless. However, it was not always that way. Once, Possum's tail was covered in long, luxurious fur, and Possum was very proud of it. Possum was always singing about how beautiful his tail was and showing it off at dances, and every morning he sat outside his lodge and combed his tail until the fur shone in the sun.

Rabbit soon became very tired of Possum showing off his fine tail.

"That Possum," Rabbit said. "Always bragging about his tail, and waving it about in the air, and combing it where everyone can see. Someone needs to take him down a peg."

Now, Rabbit was jealous of Possum's tail because Rabbit only had a small, stubby tail. This was because Rabbit once argued with Bear, and Bear pulled off Rabbit's fine, long tail. Everyone knew what had happened to Rabbit, and he couldn't stand to be reminded of what a lovely tail he'd had before Bear got his paws on it. Rabbit decided that he would play a trick on Possum—a trick that would stop him singing and bragging about his tail forever.

Not long after Rabbit decided to play his trick, the animals decided it was time for them to have a great council and dance. Rabbit was the messenger, so he went to each of the animals and told them when the council and dance would be held.

When Rabbit came to Possum's lodge and told him about the council and dance, Possum said, "Well, I guess I'll come, but I'll only be there if I have a special seat out in front. I want to spread out my lovely tail so that everyone can admire it."

"Oh, I think that can be arranged," Rabbit said. "And I'll not only make sure you get the best seat—I'll even send someone to help you comb your tail so that it will be the most beautiful thing anyone has ever seen."

"That is splendid!" Possum said. "I will surely come to the council now. I can't wait to show off my tail!"

"Oh, you're going to show it off all right," Rabbit said to himself as he hopped away from Possum's lodge. "Just not in the way you think."

Next, Rabbit went to Cricket's lodge. He invited Cricket to the council and dance and asked him to help with a little trick he had planned.

"I'll certainly come to the council and dance," Cricket said. "Tell me what you have in mind for your trick, and I'll see to it that it gets done."

Rabbit told Cricket what to do, and then he hopped away to tell the rest of the animals about the council.

In the morning, Cricket went to Possum's lodge. Possum was already sitting outside and had just begun to comb his tail.

"Good morning, Possum," Cricket said. "My, what a lovely tail you have! Someone should help you get it ready for the council this evening. It would be a shame if it weren't absolutely perfect when everyone sees it."

"Just so," Possum said. "Would you be willing to help?"

"Certainly!" Cricket said, and so Possum handed Cricket his comb and then laid down and closed his eyes to enjoy having his tail combed by someone else.

Cricket combed out Possum's tail so that it shone even more brightly than it ever had before. When he was done, he said to Possum, "It would be a shame if any little bit of fur came out of place before the council. What if I tied it up so that it stays just as perfect as it is now? You can remove the threads when you get to the council place and show everyone your perfect tail."

"That is a splendid idea, Cricket!" Possum said. "Please do tie up my tail."

Cricket got some fine thread and began wrapping it around Possum's tail. But as he did so, he snipped off every last hair at the roots. Cricket did this so gently that Possum didn't notice at all, and the thread held everything in place, so the tail looked as it always did, except wrapped up in thread.

That evening, Possum went to the council, his tail still wrapped up in the thread. Rabbit greeted him and showed him to a special seat, just as he had promised. Soon it came time for Possum to dance. He pulled the thread off his tail, but he was so intent on dancing his very best and showing off his tail that he didn't notice all the fur falling to the ground, leaving his tail as bare as bare could be.

Possum went into the center of the circle and began to dance and sing.

"My tail is the most beautiful," he sang, not noticing that all the other animals were shouting at him because they had seen all the fur fall off his tail.

Possum sang and danced some more.

"My tail has the most shining fur. The fur has the best color."

Again, the animals shouted at Possum, but he still didn't notice.

"Look at my tail!" Possum sang. "It's the best tail in the world!"

Finally, Possum had to stop singing and pay attention to the other animals because now the animals were all laughing so hard at Possum's bare tail that their sides hurt.

Possum looked down, and instead of a beautiful tail covered in soft, fine fur, there was this naked thing without a single hair on it. It looked just like a lizard's tail! Possum was astonished and very ashamed. So much so that he couldn't even finish his dance. Instead, he flopped down on the ground and rolled over onto his back, with a grin on his face. And that is why opossums now roll over and play dead if they are caught by surprise.

Kanati and Selu

Kanati and Selu were man and wife, and they lived very happily together. Kanati's name meant "Lucky Hunter," and every time he went out to hunt, he came home with something good to eat. Selu's name meant "Corn," and she grew many good things in her garden. Selu also prepared the meat that Kanati brought home. When she was done butchering it, she would go to the river and wash the blood off the meat in the flowing water.

Kanati and Selu had one child, a son. The boy was quite young and spent most of his days playing in the woods near his family's home, or along the riverbank. For several days in a row, Kanati and Selu heard their son laughing and talking with someone down near the river. It sounded like he was playing with another child, but no other families were living nearby.

Finally, the boy's parents decided to find out what was going on.

Kanati asked him, "Who is it that you play with every day, down near the river?"

"Oh, there's another little boy there," the child said. "He comes up out of the river. He says he's my older brother, but his mother threw him away. When we are done playing, he goes back into the river."

When Kanati and Selu heard this, they knew exactly where the strange boy was from. He had been born from the blood that Selu had washed into the river when she prepared the meat that Kanati brought home.

For the next few days, Kanati and Selu tried to get a glimpse of the boy that came out of the river, but he always managed to slip away right before they arrived.

Kanati then went to his son and said, "Next time the boy from the river comes to play with you, tell him that you want to wrestle with him. While you are wrestling, wrap your arms tight around him and hold him fast. When you have him pinned, call me, and I will come to you."

In the morning, Kanati and Selu's son went down by the river to play, as he always did. Kanati and Selu waited near the lodge to see whether their son would call for them. Sure enough, they soon heard their child calling loudly for his father. Kanati and Selu ran down to the riverbank. There they saw their son holding tightly to another child, who was about the same size as their boy. The other child was trying hard to get away, but Kanati and Selu's son quickly held him.

When the child from the river saw Selu, he shouted, "Leave me alone! Let me go! You didn't want me. You threw me away. You threw me into the river!"

Kanati and Selu took the strange river boy by the hand and dragged him back to their lodge. Because he seemed always to want to escape, Kanati and Selu kept him locked inside the lodge.

After many days, the child from the river began to calm down and seemed willing to live with his new family. Kanati and Selu adopted him as their son and called him Wild Boy. But even though Wild Boy stopped trying to escape, his nature was still untamed, and he frequently got up to mischief, coming up with cunning plans and getting his brother to help him carry them out.

One day, Wild Boy and his brother sat together on the riverbank.

Wild Boy said, "Father always brings home game every morning. He never comes home empty-handed. But I've never once seen a deer or turkey or rabbit anywhere around here. I wonder where the animals come from?"

"I don't know," Wild Boy's brother said. "He never told me, and I've never asked."

"Let's follow him tomorrow," Wild Boy said. "I want to find out where all that meat comes from."

In the morning, Kanati went out to hunt as usual. The boys pretended to be uninterested in where their father was going, but as soon as they thought he wouldn't notice them following, they crept along the path behind him. They followed until Kanati entered a swamp.

Wild Boy said to his brother, "Stay here. I'm going to go with Father."

Then Wild Boy changed himself into a bit of bird's down and alighted on Kanati's shoulder. Wild Boy rode along until Kanati stopped at a pond where some reeds were growing. Kanati picked some of the reeds and fixed arrowheads and feathers to them to make arrows. When he had enough arrows, he walked out of the swamp.

At the edge of the swamp, the wind rose, blowing Wild Boy in his bird-down shape off his father's shoulder.

Wild Boy then took his human form again and went to find his brother.

"What did you find?" the other boy asked when Wild Boy arrived at the place he was hiding.

"I'm not sure," Wild Boy said. "Father took some reeds and put some feathers on one end and something pointy on the other. I don't know what those are for, but I want to find out. Come on—I know which way Father went. We can probably still follow him if we're quick."

The boys soon found their father's trail and could see him walking steadily up the mountain through the trees. The boys walked as quietly as they could and kept well out of sight.

Finally, Kanati came to a place where the mountain's stone face rose into the sky, and where there were many large rocks piled against it. Kanati moved one of the large rocks aside, and out sprang a deer. Kanati nocked an arrow to his bow and shot the deer. Then he closed up the hole in the mountain, put the deer on his shoulders, and headed for home.

"Look at that!" Wild Boy said. "He just comes here, lets an animal out, kills it, and then comes home. That's why he's such a good hunter—he has all the game shut inside the mountain."

"Yes," Wild Boy's brother said, "but if we don't get home before he does, he'll be suspicious, and we'll both be in terrible trouble if he finds out that we followed him today."

"True," Wild Boy said. "Let's run. I know a shortcut through the forest."

The boys ran as fast as they could and arrived home just moments before their father.

"Why are you both so out of breath?" Kanati said when he saw the boys panting in front of the lodge.

"Oh, we just had a race to see who could get from the river to home the fastest," said Wild Boy. "I won, of course."

The boys waited for a few days before going back to the hole where the animals were held. They waited until their parents weren't watching and then followed the trail their father had taken through the forest and up the mountain. They found the stone that covered the hole and moved it aside. Suddenly, out of the hole streamed hundreds and hundreds of animals and birds. Deer, raccoons, opossums, and rabbits went jumping and running past. Turkeys, pigeons, pheasants, and all manner of other birds flew out of the hole and into the trees. The boys covered the hole back up, but by the time they had rolled the heavy stone back into place, it was too late. All the birds and animals had gone.

Back at the lodge, Kanati heard a noise like thunder coming from the direction of the mountain. He looked up and saw great clouds of birds flying up into the sky and scattering in every direction. Kanati called for his children, but they didn't answer. Then Kanati knew what had happened: his naughty boys had followed him one day and found the hole where he kept the birds and animals. Kanati ran to the place where the hole was, arriving just as the boys were putting the stone back over the hole.

Kanati said nothing to the two boys, who stood next to the hole, hanging their heads in shame. Kanati moved the stone aside and went into the hole. Inside the hole were four large jars, covered tightly with lids. Kanati kicked over the jars one by one, and out of the jars came all kinds of insects. Fleas, lice, wasps, hornets, and biting gnats came streaming out of the hole. Many of them alit on the boys and began to sting and bite them. Kanati did nothing; he allowed the boys to be punished by the stings and the bites.

When he thought they had suffered enough, Kanati chased away the insects and sat the boys down to talk.

"What you have done is very bad indeed," he said. "Before you opened the hole, all I had to do was come up here and let out an animal or a bird or two, and then we'd have plenty to eat. But now that you've let out all the birds and animals, I won't be able to get them back in there. From now on, when we hunt, we'll have to go looking for game, and there might be some days when we don't find any. Go home now, and try to stay out of trouble. I'll see whether I can catch something for dinner, but that might not be possible."

The boys went home, not saying a word to each other all the long way back to the lodge. When they arrived, they were very tired and hungry.

"Is there anything to eat, Mother?" Wild Boy said.

"There is no meat because Father hasn't come back from hunting yet," Selu said. "But maybe I can cook you something else. Rest here while I go find some food." Then Selu picked up a basket and left the lodge.

"I wonder where she gets all the grain, fruit, and vegetables she serves us." Wild Boy said. "Maybe we should follow her and find out."

"Haven't you learned anything?" Wild Boy's brother said. "You just watch: If we follow her and see what happens wherever it is that she goes, something horrible will happen, just like it happened with the animals and birds. And then we'll really be hungry."

"Maybe something will happen, maybe it won't," Wild Boy said. "You don't have to come with me if you're so frightened. I can find things out by myself."

In the end, Wild Boy's brother went along because he was stung by being called a coward. The two boys crept after their mother, who walked through the forest carrying the empty basket.

Finally, she arrived at a storehouse that had but one door and no windows, and that had been built upon tall stilts so that the animals couldn't get into it. Selu climbed up the ladder and went into the storehouse with her basket. Once she had gone inside, the boys followed and picked a hole in the clay that had been used to caulk between the logs that made the floor of the storehouse.

"Why, it's completely empty!" Wild Boy whispered to his brother.

"That is certainly strange," the other boy said, who couldn't see as well into the room as Wild Boy could. "What is she doing now?"

"She's rubbing her belly. Oh!"

"What happened?"

"When she rubbed her belly, the basket filled halfway with corn! Wait, she's rubbing under her armpits now. Oh!" Wild Boy said.

"What happened this time?"

"The other half of the basket filled up with beans!"

"How is that even possible?"

"I think our mother must be a witch," Wild Boy said. "We mustn't eat anything out of that basket. It's surely poisonous."

"What are we going to do?"

"Right now, we're going to get down and hide because Mother is getting ready to leave the storehouse."

The two boys scrambled down the ladder and hid behind some bushes. They waited until their mother had left and then started to walk home.

"If our mother is a witch," Wild Boy said, "we should kill her. It won't do to have a witch living in our lodge."

"No, indeed," the other boy said.

The boys found heavy branches to use as clubs and went into the lodge, where Selu was waiting for them.

"I know what you are thinking," she said, "and I can't stop you from carrying out your plan. But if you are wise, you will follow my instructions. When you have killed me, go outside the lodge and clear a big, circular patch of ground. Drag my body around the circle seven times. Then drag my body seven times across the middle of the circle. Stay up all night to watch, and in the morning, there will be plenty of corn for you to eat."

The boys then killed their mother with their clubs and cut off her head with a sharp knife. They put her head on top of the lodge, facing west.

"Keep a lookout for your husband," the boys said to Selu's head.

Then, they cleared a space in front of the lodge, but instead of clearing it thoroughly, they only cleared seven small patches, and this is why corn grows only in some parts of the world and not in others. The boys took Selu's body and dragged it around the circle, and wherever drops of her blood landed, young corn plants sprouted up. But the boys didn't follow their mother's instructions properly. Instead of dragging her seven times, they only dragged her twice, which is why a crop of corn must be worked twice, and not just once. When that work was done, the boys sat down to keep watch over the corn that had sprouted in the clearing.

While the two boys were watching the corn, Kanati came home.

"Where is your mother?" he asked the two boys.

"She was a witch, so we killed her," Wild Boy said.

"Yes. We put her head up on the top of the lodge," Wild Boy's brother said.

Kanati looked up at the top of the lodge, and there he saw the head of his dead wife.

He became very angry and said, "I cannot stay here with you. You don't know how to behave. I am going to the Wolf people now."

Kanati began to leave the clearing, but before he had gone very far, Wild Boy turned himself into a little tuft of down and settled on his father's shoulder.

Kanati never noticed the piece of down but kept walking on until he arrived where the Wolf people lived. When he arrived, he found the Wolf people were already gathered together to have a council.

The chief of the Wolf people saw Kanati arrive and said, "Welcome, stranger. Won't you tell us why you are here?"

"I am here because both of my sons are very bad people," Kanati said. "Something must be done about them. In seven days, please go to my lodge and play ball with those boys."

"We will go," the chief of the Wolf people said.

When Kanati heard the chief's promise, he left the place of the Wolf people. But he didn't go back home; instead, he kept walking on.

Now, when Kanati said "go play ball," what he really meant was "go and kill the boys," and the Wolf chief understood this. Wild Boy, who was still on his father's shoulder in the form of down, heard everything that had been said, and he understood what "go play ball" meant too.

Wild Boy allowed himself to float away from his father's shoulder and be carried away by the smoke from the council fire. Up, up, up, he floated, right through the smoke hole in the lodge. He floated over the roof of the lodge and then settled on the ground.

Wild Boy changed back into his human form and ran back home as fast as he could.

"We are in big trouble," Wild Boy said to his brother when he finally arrived home. "Father went to the Wolf people and asked them to come here and eat us. I know what we need to do to get ready. Come with me."

Wild Boy and his brother went outside the lodge, where they ran around it in a wide circle. They ran many times, to make a trail that stayed in the soft ground. They didn't close the circle, but rather, left one small piece open on the side that faced the direction the Wolf people would be coming from. Then the boys made themselves many arrows. They grouped them into four bunches and placed each bunch at intervals around the outside of the circle. Then they took their bows and hid behind some trees to wait for the Wolves to come.

A couple of days later, the Wolves arrived. They didn't see the trail the boys had made around the lodge, but they did go in through the opening, just as Wild Boy had said they would. As soon as the Wolves went through that gap, a great fence of briars and branches grew up along the trail that the boys had trampled into the ground. The boys then took their bows and used the arrows they had staged earlier to start killing the Wolves, who could not jump over the fence because it was too high. A few of the Wolves managed to escape through the opening and ran into the nearby swamp.

Wild Boy and his brother followed them, and when they reached the edge of the swamp, they both ran in circles around it. Wherever Wild Boy and his brother ran, flames sprang up in their tracks. The fire burned its way into the swamp and killed all the Wolves except for two or three, who managed to escape. They became the ancestors of all the wolves that are in the world today.

The boys continued to live at their parents' lodge, harvesting the corn that grew up in the clearing and hunting for game in the forest. They sometimes made bread from the corn, and soon other people began to hear of the wonderful bread that these two boys made. One day, some strangers came to the lodge to speak to the boys.

"We have heard about your bread," the strangers said, "and we were hoping you would give us some."

"We'll do better than that," the boys said. "Here are seven grains of corn. Plant one every night on your way home, and watch over them all night. In the morning, you'll have plenty of corn that you can use to make bread for yourselves."

The strangers thanked the boys and returned home, a journey that took them seven days. At the end of the first day, they made camp and planted one of the seeds. They watched over the seed, and in the morning, seven tall stalks of corn were growing where the seed had been planted. They harvested the corn and went on their way. Each night when they made camp, they planted seeds of corn and watched over them, and each morning, even more corn was growing for them to harvest.

Now, the journey home was a long and weary one, and after five nights without sleep, the people were very tired. They planted the corn but were not able to keep their eyes open. They fell asleep, and in the morning, they found that no corn had grown at all. They brought home all the corn they had harvested and showed the people how to plant and harvest it, but because they had failed to watch over the seeds every night, it now takes many months for a crop to grow and ripen—where before it took only one night.

By the time the strangers came to visit the boys, Kanati had been gone for many months and had not returned.

"I think we should try to find Father," Wild Boy said.

"Yes," his brother said. "Let's try to find him."

Wild Boy took a wheel and rolled it to the west. Not long after, the wheel came back. Wild Boy took the wheel and rolled it to the north and south, and each time the wheel returned. Wild Boy then rolled the wheel to the east. The boys waited and waited, but the wheel did not come back.

"That is the direction we must look," Wild Boy said, so the brothers made ready and then set out eastward to find their father.

After many days of walking, the boys saw Kanati walking up ahead, with a small dog at his heels. The boys knew for certain that this was Kanati because the little dog was the wheel they had rolled. When it found Kanati, it turned itself into a dog and followed him everywhere.

The boys ran up to Kanati. Kanati stopped and looked at them.

Then, he said, "You are very bad boys. What are you doing here? Why are you following me?"

"We are men, and we go where we please," the boys replied.

"Do you intend to travel with me?"

"Yes."

"Very well. You may travel with me. But you have to go wherever I lead you."

The boys agreed, and so the three of them resumed their journey. After a time, they came to the edge of a swamp.

"Don't go in there," Kanati said. "There's something very dangerous that lives in that swamp."

Kanati resumed his journey, but the boys halted for a bit at the edge of the swamp.

"Let's go see what's in there," Wild Boy said. "I bet it's not half as bad as Father says it is."

The boys went into the swamp. They hadn't gone far when they found a giant panther, asleep. The boys took their bows and shot many arrows into the panther, but they could not kill it, and the panther paid them no attention. The boys gave up and left the swamp.

They caught up with Kanati, who said, "Well, did you find the dangerous thing?"

"We did. But it didn't hurt us at all, because we are men and we are not afraid."

Kanati was surprised by this news, but he didn't say anything. Instead, he resumed his journey, and the boys followed him.

After more walking, Kanati stopped and pointed. "See that place over there? That's a place where cannibals live. You want to stay away from there because if you go near, the cannibals will catch you and eat you."

Of course, no sooner had the words left Kanati's mouth than the boys wanted to go and see the cannibal village. They headed in the direction Kanati had indicated, and on the way, they came across a tree that had been struck by lightning.

"Take some of those burnt splinters," Wild Boy told his brother. "They'll come in useful later. I'll tell you what to do with them on our way to the cannibal village."

It didn't take long before the cannibals saw the two boys approaching. They ran up to the boys, captured them, and brought them back to their village.

"Everybody come and see what fine, fat boys we have caught!" the chief of the cannibals said. "Tonight, we eat well. Prepare for the feast!"

The cannibals made a great fire and put a big cauldron full of water over it. When the water was boiling, they grabbed Wild Boy and put him into the pot and put on the lid. But before Wild Boy went into the water, his brother knelt and put the splinters he had gathered from the tree into the fire. Then the cannibals put the other boy into the pot as well.

After some time, the chief of the cannibals said, "I think the meat should be ready now. Let's eat!"

All the cannibals gathered around, bowls at the ready to get their share. The chief took the lid off the pot, but instead of a nicely boiled dinner, a great ball of lightning was inside. The lightning exploded out of the pot, bolts flying everywhere. The lightning struck all of the cannibals, and soon they were all dead. Then the lightning gathered itself together and went up and out of the smoke hole. When the lightning disappeared, Wild Boy and his brother were standing there in the middle of the village as if nothing had happened.

The boys went looking for their father, and soon they caught up to him. Kanati was very surprised to see them.

"What, you're still alive?" he said.

"Of course we are," the boys said.

"Didn't you find the cannibal village?"

"Yes, we did, but we are men, and we are not afraid, so they did us no harm."

Kanati asked no more questions, but instead resumed his journey, and the boys followed him. This time, though, Kanati began walking very fast, and the boys couldn't keep up with him. They followed his trail, which ended at the place where the sun rises, at the very edge of the world. There the boys found Kanati and Selu.

"Come and join us," Selu said. "You can rest here a while, but you can't stay. This isn't a place for you. Your place is in the west, where the sun goes down. After you have rested, you need to go to the western edge of the world, which will be your new home."

The boys stayed with their parents for seven days, and then they set out for the edge of the world where the sun sets. They talked together as they walked along, and people far away heard their conversations, which sounded to them like the rumbling of thunder. The boys kept walking until they got to the edge of the world where the sun sets, and there they made their home.

Now, after the boys let all the animals and birds out of the hole in the mountain many years earlier, life became very hard for the people. There came a time when even the best hunters came home empty-handed, day after day.

"We will starve if this goes on much longer," the people said. "What can we do?"

One wise man said, "Send someone to the west to get the Thunder Boys. They'll be able to help us."

Messengers went to the Thunder Boys to ask for help. The boys readily agreed, and they journeyed to the place where the people lived.

When they got there, they said to the people, "We will call the deer for you. Have your bows ready."

Then the boys went into the townhouse, where the people had their feasts and their councils, and they began to sing. The boys sang their first song, and a sound like a roaring wind came from the northwest. The boys kept singing, and the noise got louder with each song. Just as the boys began their seventh song, a whole herd of deer came out of the forest. The people stood ready with their bows, as they had been told to do, and soon they had killed many deer, enough to feed the people for a long time.

The boys then said to the people, "We need to go back to our home. Once we get there, you will never see us again, but before we go, we will teach you our songs so that you can call the deer yourselves."

The boys taught the people all seven songs, but as the years passed, the songs became forgotten, all except for two, and these are the songs hunters still sing today when they want to catch deer.

The Tlanuwa and the Uktena

The Tlanuwa were great birds of prey that lived long, long ago. Their bodies were as long as a man is tall, and their wingspan was huge to match. They had sharp beaks and long talons, and they flew over the land every day looking for food for themselves and their young. The Tlanuwa were not particular about what they ate. Dogs would do just as well as deer, and if other animals weren't available, the Tlanuwa would swoop down and snatch up human children and bring them back to their nest to eat.

The Tlanuwa made their nest along the Little Tennessee River, on a high cliff where there was a cave. The cliff was sheer up to where the cave was, and the cave was protected from above by a rocky overhang that prevented anyone from climbing down to the nest. The people longed to rid themselves of these monstrous birds, but no matter how they tried, they were unable. Many brave men tried to climb up the cliff, but none could make it to the nest. Next, they tried waiting on the riverbank, bows at the ready. They shot arrows at the birds when they flew out to hunt, but it was no use: the arrows merely bounced off the birds' feathers.

Finally, the people went to the wisest medicine man they knew.

"Please help us," they said. "The Tlanuwa have taken so many of our children, and they're eating all the deer. Soon we will have neither children nor food, and we will die of starvation and sorrow."

"I know of the Tlanuwa," the medicine man said. "And I think I know how to deal with them, but I will need some of you to help me."

Several of the men readily agreed to help, and so the medicine man started the work he needed to do to prepare for his attack on the Tlanuwa's nest. First, the medicine man took strips of linn bark and made a long rope out of it. At the end of the rope, there were loops that he could put his feet into. Then he took a sturdy branch and carved it into a staff with a hook on one end. When the rope and staff were complete, the medicine man and his helpers climbed up to the top of the cliff, where they waited until the adult birds left to go hunting.

As soon as the adult birds left the cave, the medicine man told his helpers to hold the rope, and lower him down slowly, and then wait for him to tug on the rope to let them know he was ready to be pulled back up. The medicine man put his feet into the loops, and his helpers lowered him slowly and carefully over the edge of the overhang. Then the medicine man began to swing himself on the rope, back and forth, until he could hook his staff onto part of the wall of the cave where the nest was. Using the staff, he pulled himself onto the shelf and went over to the nest.

Inside the nest were four chicks. They had hatched only a few days ago, and so were still quite small, only about as big as a baby deer. The medicine man grabbed the nestlings one by one and threw them into the river below, where they were eaten by the Uktena, a great serpent who lived in the water. No sooner had the Uktena swallowed the nestlings than the medicine man saw the two parent birds flying back to the nest. He tugged on the rope, and his helpers pulled him back up just in time.

The Tlanuwa were very angry to find their nest empty. They flew out of the cave and circled in the air high above the river, screaming their rage into the sky. In the river below, the Uktena heard the noise the Tlanuwa were making, so he poked his head out of the water to see what was going on. The Tlanuwa saw the Uktena, and they immediately swooped down and snatched up the great snake in their talons. They ripped the Uktena to shreds in midair, and wherever a piece of the snake's body landed, it carved a hole in the rock. Those holes are still there today.

Two Tales of Snake Transformations

The Snake Boy

Once there was a boy who was the best in the village at hunting birds. Whenever he went out, he always came back with plenty of birds, which he would give to his grandmother. Everyone else in the village was jealous of the boy, both of his skill and of the fact that he would only share his catch with his grandmother. The villagers treated him so spitefully that he resolved to leave his village forever.

On the morning that the boy decided to start his journey, his grandmother prepared breakfast for him, but he would not eat.

"I can eat nothing today, Grandmother," he said, "because I am going on a great journey, and I need to fast so that I will be ready for whatever happens. But you must not grieve—I will be going somewhere safe, and I will be well. I love you always."

The boy then went out into the forest, where he spent the day.

In the evening, he returned with a pair of deer antlers he had found in the woods. Instead of going home, he went inside the winter house, where he found his grandmother waiting for him.

"Grandmother, I must sleep alone here tonight," the boy said.

The grandmother was sad, but she left the boy alone as he wished and went to sleep in another of her family's houses.

At daybreak, the grandmother rose and went to the winter house where her grandson had slept. She peeked through the door and what should she see but an enormous serpent, with horns on its head and two human legs!

"Grandmother, do not be afraid," the serpent said. "It is I, your grandson. I beg you to leave now. You have already seen too much."

The grandmother stepped away from the door but kept watch over the winter house. Many hours passed. When the sun was high in the sky, the door of the winter house opened, and a great uktena came slithering out. The uktena was so big that it took an hour for it to exit the house completely.

After the uktena left, it went through the village, hissing as it went. All the villagers were frightened and ran away, except for the grandmother, who knew who the uktena really was. The uktena slithered its way through the village and went down to the river, where it slid into the water and disappeared. The great serpent was so heavy that it left behind a deep channel in the ground along the path that it had taken.

The grandmother was heartbroken that her grandson had turned himself into an uktena and had gone to live in the river. She mourned for a very long time, and finally, the rest of the family became very impatient with her sadness.

"You saw where he went," they said. "If you miss him that much, why don't you throw yourself into the river and join him?"

"Very well," the grandmother said.

She left the village, following the track the serpent had made with its body. She arrived at the riverbank, but she never stopped walking. She walked into the water and kept walking until she disappeared into the deep running water.

Now, that was not the last time the people saw the grandmother. One day, a fisherman was casting his net on the riverbank, and he happened to look toward a large rock that rose out of the water a little way downstream. There he saw the grandmother, looking as she always did, sitting on the rock in the sun. As soon as the grandmother noticed the fisherman staring at her, she jumped in the water and was gone.

The Snake Man

Two hunters left their village early in the morning to see whether they might find some game to bring home. They followed many tracks and moved quietly, but no matter where they went, they found nothing but squirrels.

"I'm hungry," one hunter said, "and I swear those squirrels are taunting me. I'm going to catch some of them and have a fine feast tonight."

"Don't do it!" his companion said. "You know it's forbidden to eat squirrels. Something terrible will happen to you if you do."

"Nothing is going to happen. That's just a tale they made up to frighten children. I'm going to dress these squirrels and roast them, and then I'm going to eat them. There's plenty for both of us if you want to join me."

"No, thank you. Sometimes tales that are made up to frighten children actually mean what they say. I'd rather go hungry than find out what would happen if I ate squirrel."

The hunter laughed. "All right. Suit yourself."

The hunter proceeded to dress and cook the squirrels, which he ate hungrily. Meanwhile, his companion laid down and made ready for sleep. His back was turned to his friend so that he wouldn't be tempted to eat the squirrels too. It was hard to resist because the sizzling meat smelled so good, but the companion was steadfast, and eventually, he went to sleep—even though his stomach rumbled with hunger.

In the middle of the night, the companion was roused by the sound of agonized groaning. He opened his eyes and sat up, and on the other side of the fire, he saw his friend, writhing and moaning in agony. But that wasn't all: the hunter's legs had already stuck themselves together and were covered with shining green scales. He was turning into a giant serpent!

The companion watched in horror as his friend slowly turned into a giant serpent. There was nothing he could do to help, and soon the transformation was complete. In the place of the hunter, there was a great water snake. The snake looked once at the companion and then slithered off into the river. It was never seen again.

The Daughter of the Sun

As everyone knows, the Sun lives on the other side of the vault of the sky, but her daughter lives below it, right in the middle. Every day, the Sun climbs the great vault of the sky, starting in the east, and then she walks down the other side and goes to sleep in the west. When she gets to the middle of the sky, she likes to stop and visit with her daughter, and they share a meal.

Now, the Sun loved her daughter very much, but she wasn't as fond of the people who lived down on the earth.

One day, she couldn't bear it any longer, so she complained to the Moon, "Those people are just so ugly. Every time they look at me, they scrunch up their faces and squint. None of them will even bother to look at me properly. It's terribly ungrateful, considering all I do for them."

"I don't know what you're talking about," the Moon said. "Whenever they look at me, they smile. I find the people quite pleasant indeed."

Upon hearing that the Moon received such greetings from the people, Sun's jealously grew stronger. Finally, she decided that the best way to solve the problem would be to kill all the people. Every day, as she got close to her daughter's house, she sent down rays that carried a fever. Soon all the people were very sick, and many of them died. But still, the Sun did not stop; she wanted to keep sending the rays until every last person was dead.

The people were very worried.

"Everyone in our village has lost a loved one," they said, "and more people are getting sick by the day. If this keeps up, soon there will be no more people."

The people didn't know what to do. They had no power to stop the Sun. They held a council, and it was decided that they would go and ask the Little Men for help. The Little Men had magic powers, and they were on friendly terms with the people.

When the Little Men heard what the Sun was doing, they said, "Oh, dear. There's really only one way you can save yourselves. You'll have to kill the Sun."

"We don't know how to do that," the people said. "We don't even know how to get up to her house."

"Don't worry. We know what to do. Send us two of your bravest warriors tomorrow morning, and we'll get your problem solved."

In the morning, the two bravest warriors went to see the Little Men. The Little Men changed the men into snakes. One became a hognose snake, while the other was turned into a copperhead.

"Go to the house where the Sun's daughter lives," the Little Men said. "The Sun goes there for a meal every day at noon. If you wait next to the door, you can bite her when she arrives. Then she'll die, and you'll be free of the fever."

The two snakes slithered up into the sky and waited near the house of the Sun's daughter. At midday, the Sun arrived. The hognose snake was first to strike, but the Sun's light was so bright that he was blinded. All he could do was flop over on his back and spit out smelly slime.

The Sun saw the snake and smelled the slime.

"Oh, you disgusting thing," she said and nudged it away from the door with her toe.

The copperhead was so frightened by what had happened to the hognose snake that he slithered back home without even trying to bite. The hognose snake followed later—when he woke up from his fainting spell.

The two men went to visit the Little Men the next day. They explained what had happened.

"The Sun was too powerful," they said. "We couldn't even get close to her. Change us into some other kind of snake, one that can get close to the Sun."

This time, the Little Men changed one man into an uktena, and the other into a rattlesnake. The two snakes slithered back up to the house of the Sun's daughter and lay in wait for the Sun. As midday neared, the two snakes became very anxious. The rattlesnake coiled itself up in readiness to strike.

"I'm not going to miss this time," he said. "I'm so fast that the Sun won't even know what hit her."

Suddenly, the Sun's daughter opened the door of her house and stepped outside to see whether her mother was coming. The rattlesnake was so on edge that he didn't even think to make sure whom he was biting. He struck as fast as lightning, and after only a few minutes, the Sun's daughter was dead.

"Look what you did!" the uktena said. "We were supposed to kill the Sun, not this young woman. What are we going to do now?"

The rattlesnake was so ashamed of his mistake that he couldn't even reply. He slithered back home and asked the Little Men to change him back into a man. The uktena went home, too; he didn't want to be caught near the house when the Sun found out that her daughter had been killed by a snake bite.

The Sun finally arrived at her daughter's house. There on the threshold lay the body of the young woman. The Sun tried to revive her, but it was too late. Her daughter was dead. The Sun went into her daughter's house and shut the door. The world instantly became dark, and it stayed dark because the Sun would not come out. Instead, she stayed inside the house, grieving for her dead child.

Now the people had a different problem to solve. The fever had gone away, but if the world stayed dark, the plants and animals would begin to die. Soon there would be no food. So, the people went to the Little People and asked for help again.

"Since you're the ones who killed the Sun's daughter, you must be the ones to bring her back," the Little Men said. "You need to send seven men to the Ghost Country to find the Sun's daughter and bring her home to her mother."

The people chose seven brave men to go to the Ghost Country. The Little Men gave each man a rod made of sourwood. They also gave the seven men one large box.

"Here is what you must do," the Little Men said. "When you get to the Ghost Country, you will find that the ghosts are all having a dance. The Sun's daughter will be there, and she will be dancing too. As the dance circle comes around to where you are, you must strike the Sun's daughter with your sourwood rods until she falls down. Then you must pick her up and put her in the box. Close the lid tightly and then bring her back to her mother. But remember: you must not lift the lid until you get to the house where the Sun is, or the young woman will be lost forever."

The men promised to follow the instructions carefully and departed for the Ghost Country.

When they arrived, they found that the ghosts were all having a dance, just as the Little Men said they would. The men watched the dance for a while, and when they picked out the Sun's daughter from among the dancers, they got ready to strike her. Each time she went past one of the men, they hit her with their rods, and soon she fell to the ground. The men rushed over to her, picked her up, and put her in the box. The men picked up the box and started the long walk back to the Sun's daughter's house, where the Sun still sat grieving and refusing to shine.

As the men walked along carrying the box, the Sun's daughter awoke. After discovering that she had been imprisoned inside a box, she could not open the lid.

She banged on it with her fist and shouted, "Let me out! Please let me out!"

The men refused to listen and just kept walking.

For the rest of the journey, Sun's daughter begged the men to let her out.

"Please let me out! I can't breathe in here. Or if you won't let me out, at least open the lid a little way so that some fresh air can get in."

As the men were approaching the Sun's daughter's house, the pleas of the young woman became so piteous that they relented.

"Surely it won't hurt to open the box just a crack," they said. "We're so close to her house, and she's in such distress."

The men put the box down and lifted the lid just the tiniest crack. They heard a fluttering sound from inside the box. Something flew out of the box and into the bushes. The men couldn't see what it was, but they heard the sound of a redbird calling from the bushes.

The men picked the box up and continued their journey, but when they got to the house and opened the box, it was empty. The soul of the Sun's daughter had turned itself into a redbird and flown away when the men opened the box. This was a disaster not only for the Sun but also for all people because if the men had followed the instructions and kept the box shut, it would have been possible for us to visit the Ghost Country and bring our loved ones back to life. But because they opened the box too early, whenever someone dies, they are gone forever.

Now, the men had stopped by the Sun's daughter's house on the way to the Ghost Country, to let the Sun know that they were going to try to get her daughter back. The Sun had been very happy when she'd heard that news and had waited with great excitement at the prospect of getting to see her daughter again. But when the men opened the box and found it empty, the Sun began to wail and weep great tears. She wept so much that the earth became flooded, and the people began to drown.

So, the people decided to send their most beautiful young men and young women to sing and dance for the Sun, hoping that the music and dancing would cheer her up so that she would stop crying and shine again. The young people sang and danced in the best way they knew how, but nothing they did seemed to make any difference. Finally, the drummer started playing a different way, and the Sun stopped crying. She looked up at the dancers and listened to the song.

She watched the dance for a little while, and then she smiled, having forgotten her grief.

The Ball Game of the Birds and Animals

There came a time when the animals challenged the birds to a ball game.

"This will prove that we're better than the birds," the animals said. "There's no way such small creatures can stand against us. Anyway, they're practically half feathers and no muscle at all. Beating them will be easy."

The birds accepted the challenge, and a place and time for the ball game were decided between Bear, who was the captain of the animal team, and Eagle, who was the captain of the birds.

All the animals and birds were very excited about the game. Bear boasted of his great strength.

"See how I can heave these big logs around like they weigh nothing?" he said. "If I can do that, then any bird who tries to get in my way will be tossed aside the same way."

Turtle said, "I have a hard shell. Nobody is going to be able to stop me. Any blows they strike will just bounce right off, and won't hurt me at all."

"I'm faster than any other creature," Deer said. "Just give me the ball, and I'll run right to the birds' goal. Nobody will be able to catch me."

Two little mice heard about the game and wanted to play too. They went to visit Bear to see whether they could join his team.

When Bear saw the two tiny creatures, he roared with laughter. "You? Play the ball game with us? No, indeed. You'd just get trodden underfoot and be no use to us whatsoever. You just watch from the sidelines and see how real animals play ball."

Now, the animals didn't think much of the birds' team, but the birds did have Eagle on their side. They also had Hawk and the great Tlanuwa. These birds were very strong and could fly very high and fast. They had heard Bear and the other animals boasting, but they paid it no mind. The birds held their peace, thinking that deeds were better than words and that the animals would soon regret having been so boastful.

On the day of the game, the birds and animals all gathered at the field that had been chosen for the game. As Eagle was gathering his players to give them one last bit of encouragement before the game started, he suddenly heard a very small voice coming from the grass around his feet.

"Excuse me," the voice said. "We'd like to play ball too. Can we be on your team?"

Eagle looked down and saw two tiny mice. "Why don't you go and ask the animal captain? After all, you're both animals, and neither of you has wings to fly with."

"We did ask the animal captain," one of the mice said. "And he was very rude to us. He won't let us play."

"Oh, that's a shame. Let's see if we can find a way to get you some wings, and you can play for our side."

Eagle and his team went looking for things to use to make wings for the mice.

"Hey, look what I found!" Hawk said. "Here's the hide from the drum we used at the dance last night. We can make wings out of this."

Eagle and Hawk worked together to make wings out of the hide and some canes they found. They tied it onto the first mouse's little paws, which is how the first bat was made.

"Here, fly up and test your wings," Eagle said. "I'll throw you the ball, and we'll see how well you can play."

Bat (for this is what we must now call the first mouse) flew up into the air, and Eagle tossed him the ball. Bat caught it easily, and no matter how hard the other birds tried to get him to drop it, he held it fast.

Eagle was very impressed. "You're very good, even though this is the first time you've played as Bat. I think we'll be glad you're on our team."

"What are we going to do about the other mouse?" Hawk said. "There's not enough of the hide left to make him some wings."

"What if we just stretch him a bit?" Martin said. "We'll make him longer and stretch the skin between his paws. Then he'll have wings too."

The second mouse agreed, and so four large birds each took one of the mouse's paws in their beak and pulled and pulled until the second mouse was quite stretched out, and a good deal of soft, thin skin had been created on his sides. This is how the flying squirrel was made.

"How about you try your wings now?" Eagle said, and so Flying Squirrel (for this is what we must now call the second mouse) skittered up the trunk of a tree. Eagle threw the ball into the air. Flying Squirrel leaped off the branch and caught the ball in his mouth, but instead of gliding to the ground, he glided to a high branch in a neighboring tree.

"You're very good too," Eagle said. "I'm glad you asked to be on our team."

When both teams were ready to play, the signal was given, and the game began. The animals had the ball first, but they didn't keep it for long. Bear lumbered toward the tree where Flying Squirrel was waiting and tossed the ball to Deer. But Deer never caught it, because Flying Squirrel glided down and grabbed the ball with his little teeth. Then Flying Squirrel tossed the ball to Hawk, and so the birds tossed the ball back and forth among their players. This went on for some time until one of the birds dropped the ball.

"Aha!" Bear said. "Once we get that ball back, you'll never hold it again!"

But Bear never touched the ball, because Martin swooped in and caught it. Then Martin tossed the ball to Bat, who caught it and began to fly toward the goal. Even though Bat was flying close to the ground, none of the animals could touch him, because he dodged and flittered this way and that so quickly that even Deer couldn't catch him.

Finally, Bat came within range of the goal and tossed the ball in, winning the game for the birds.

Thus, Bear, Deer, and Turtle went home very humbled indeed because, for all their boasting, they hadn't even touched the ball for the whole game. The birds praised Martin for his speed and quick thinking and gave him a gourd that he could live in as a prize for saving the game for them. This is why martins live in little houses even today.

How Disease and Medicine Came to Be

Back when the world was new, and everything had only just been created, all of the plants, birds, and animals could talk, just like people, and the people lived peacefully alongside all the other creatures. But the people had many children, and soon there were so many people that it became difficult for them to find enough food. They looked around them and saw that many birds, animals, and fish looked like they might be good to eat. Plus, their fur, feathers, and skins would be useful for clothing, making drums, and other things. So, the people invented bows and arrows, knives and spears, nets and fish hooks. They went about hunting the birds and animals and fishing in the rivers and lakes. Soon, the people had plenty to eat, and ample furs, feathers, and skins. However, the birds, animals, and fish were very frightened and angry about being hunted and killed every day.

One day, the bears decided to have a council to decide what was to be done about the threat posed by the people. When the time came for the council, they all gathered in the townhouse at the foot of Kuwahi Mountain, the Mulberry Place. Old White Bear was the oldest and wisest of the animals, so he led the council. One bear suggested they make war on the people, to make them stop hunting. All the other bears agreed that this was the best plan, so they began to discuss how to go about it.

One bear stood up and said, "The people have bows and arrows, and those work very well for killing us, so let's make bows and arrows of our own and use them for hunting people."

"All right," White Bear said. "We can try that. Make a bow and some arrows, and we'll use that."

One of the bears went into the forest and found a sapling for the bow. Another bear allowed himself to be killed so that his guts could be used to make the bowstring. The bear who had proposed the bow and arrows was first to try the weapon. The bear took the bow and nocked an arrow to the string. He pulled the string back and loosed the arrow, but his long claws got in the way, and the shot went nowhere near the target.

"You should trim your claws," the other bears said, so they helped the archer bear trim his claws, and then the bear tried another shot.

This time the arrow hit the center of the target.

"Oh, this is marvelous!" one bear said. "We can make many bows and arrows and go hunt the people. Then they'll leave us alone."

"Yes, they might leave us alone," White Bear said, "but what will we bears do for food? We need to climb trees to find good things to eat, and we can't go about killing half of our people to use their guts for bowstrings. Someone else will have to find a solution."

All the bears went home.

The deer came to the townhouse next for their council. Their chief was called Little Deer.

"What shall we do about the people who hunt us and use our flesh for food and our skins for clothing?" he asked.

"I have an idea," one of the deer said. "We should tell the people that their hunters have to ask our forgiveness every time they kill one of us. Otherwise, we will give them rheumatism."

Little Deer and the others agreed that this was a good solution, so they sent messengers to the settlements where the people lived.

The messengers told the people, "When you hunt us, the hunter must ask the animal he killed for forgiveness. Every time a deer is killed, our chief, Little Deer, will be there. Little Deer is swifter than the wind, and no arrow or spear can touch him. He will ask the slain deer whether the hunter asked for pardon. If the deer says 'Yes,' Little Deer will leave without doing anything. But if the deer says 'No,' Little Deer will follow the hunter home and give him rheumatism, and soon that hunter won't be able to walk anymore. He will be in pain all the time."

The next creatures to hold a council were the snakes and fish. They decided to send the people bad dreams about slimy things and rotting fish.

"That way, they will never want to eat us, because we'll make them so disgusted," the snakes and fish said. "And sometimes, the dreams will be so bad that the people will get sick and die."

When the snakes and fish were done with their council, the birds, insects, and other small animals held theirs. The frogs complained about the people calling them ugly and kicking them, which made their backs spotty. The birds complained about the people shooting them with arrows and then plucking out their feathers and roasting them over a fire.

Then, the chipmunk spoke. "I don't think the people are all that bad. At least they don't bother my people or me."

This made the other animals so angry that they slashed at the chipmunk with their claws, and this is why chipmunks have stripes on their backs.

By the time the council was ended, the birds, insects, and small animals had decided to create many different diseases and send them to the people to make them sick. Some of the diseases could kill.

Now, for all this time, the plants had been listening to the animals' councils in the townhouse.

"We can't let the people die. They are our friends," the plants said. "We will let the people take our leaves, bark, and flowers to use for medicine so that they don't die of these awful diseases."

Thus, disease and medicine came into the world.

Although the plants gladly offer themselves up as medicine, they can no longer speak, so we have to find out what purpose they have by ourselves. The healers of the tribe can find out these purposes because they know how to listen to the plants' spirits, which tell them what to use for medicine.

Part 3: Choctaw Mythology

Captivating Myths from the Choctaw and Other Indigenous Peoples from the Southeastern United States

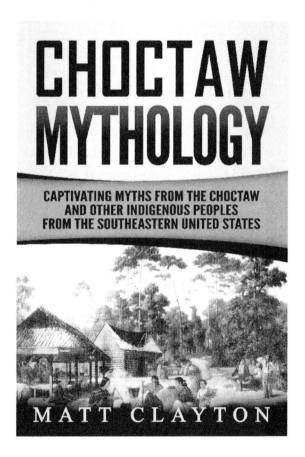

Introduction

When people think about Native Americans, the images that most likely spring to mind are Plains tribes or the desert southwest, and not those of the southeastern states. This perception is largely the result of history and white storytelling practices. White incursions into southeastern indigenous territory coupled with the forcible relocation of peoples from that region, demanded by the Removal Act of 1830, pushed these people onto reservations and out of the public consciousness, while Western films and television shows mostly focus on white settlement of the Western United States and the resulting conflict between whites and Plains tribes. However, these skewed views do not represent modern reality. Many southeastern tribes affected by the Removal Act still exist—as do other tribes throughout the United States—yet their cultures were irreparably damaged by the genocidal policies of the white state and federal governments.

Before the disruption of southeastern indigenous cultures by white settlers, the southeastern region's indigenous peoples relied on a combination of agriculture, hunting, and gathering for their sustenance. Due to their reliance on agriculture—primarily the cultivation of corn (maize), squash, and beans (the so-called "three sisters")—these tribes were sedentary, living in towns and villages that consisted of dwellings, storehouses, and a townhouse, the latter of which was the venue for councils and other important group activities.

Some of the southeastern tribes are descendants of the ancient Mississippian culture, part of whose legacy is several large mounds found in various places throughout the Mississippi Valley. The Choctaw were among these mound-builders; the story of Nanih Waiya told in this volume is a mythical relation of the origin of that particular mound, which still stands today in Winston County, Mississippi, and which in 2008 was formally ceded to the Mississippi Band of Choctaw Indians. These mounds were used as ceremonial or religious sites in some cases, while others appear to have been constructed over burials.

Many southeast peoples speak languages in the Muskogean language family, and many myths and tales also have versions that are shared among tribes. Rabbit is a trickster hero in all of these cultures, while other animals common to the region, such as turkeys and alligators, make appearances as well. Thunder beings appear in tales from both the Choctaw and Natchez peoples—only the Choctaw story is presented in this volume—while the owl acts as a villain in stories from both the Choctaw and the Caddo.

The first part of this book contains Choctaw myths and legends. In this section are stories that explain Choctaw beliefs about the origin and structure of the universe and the origin of corn, an important staple food. The alligator appears here not as a villain but as a grateful recipient of human aid, while the owl is a murderous old woman. Adventurers seek new places in the Choctaw migration legend and in the story of Tashka and Walo, two boys who journey to the home of the Sun.

The second half of the book comprises stories from six other southeastern tribes: the Seminole, Natchez, Alabama, Creek, Caddo, and Chitimacha. Animal characters such as Alligator, Rabbit, and Owl play roles here, too, the first in a just-so story about the shape of the alligator's snout, the second in his usual guise as a wily trickster, and the third as a devious man who dupes two ambitious girls into becoming his wives. Journeys to the sky country are represented by the tale of the sky maidens who come down to Earth to play ball, and in the story of the gifts of Kutnahin, a solar deity of the Chitimacha people.

Tie-snakes, which appear in a Creek legend presented below, are supernatural water-dwelling serpents that play a role in many southeastern legends and can be benevolent or malevolent. Here they are helpful, provided that the hero of the story can meet their demands. The other Creek story in this volume relies on the common folklore tropes of the man-eating beast and the child-prodigy hero, who is the only one who can defeat the villain. But regardless of the origin of the story, whether from the Choctaw, the Creek, or any of the other tribes represented here, each tale in this volume explains something important about indigenous peoples' understanding of the world and the places of the people, animals, and birds who live in it.

Part I: Choctaw Myths and Legends

The Creation of the World

When the world was new, all that existed was a flat plain and the sky above it. On the plain was a great hill called Nanih Waiya, "the sloping hill."

The Creator decided that the world needed some people, so he caused people to come out of the earth around the mound. Each person that emerged went and sat on the hill. Some say that the first people to emerge were the Muskogee, who left and went east, where they made their home. Allegedly, the Cherokees and Chickasaws came next. The Cherokees followed the Muskogees' trail, but the Muskogees had stopped to smoke tobacco on the way and accidentally caused a fire in the forest. The Cherokees could not find the Muskogees' trail, which had been burned away by the fire, so they turned north and made their home there. The Chickasaws followed the Cherokees and made their home nearby. Then the Choctaws came out of the mound, but they decided to stay right there, and so they made their home next to Nanih Waiya.

The Creator watched all the people come out of the mound and go their different ways, and when he thought the world had enough people, he stamped hard on the ground with his foot. Some people were still being formed when he did this, still coming out of the earth, but when the Creator stamped his foot, they stopped being created and died, sinking back into the ground.

The Creator gathered the people on the hill and told them that they would live forever.

"What is 'forever'? Is living forever a good thing? What happens to us when forever is over?" the people asked.

The Creator became annoyed that the people did not understand what a great gift he was offering them, so he made them mortal instead, and this is why we have death.

After the Creator made the people, a great flood came. The waters rushed and flowed all around the mound where the people were sitting. The wind blew in great gusts, causing waves to form on the waters. Soon the storm and the flood were over, and the people saw that the land was no longer a flat plain with their mound in the middle. Instead, there were hills, mountains, valleys, and riverbeds and streambeds with good, fresh water.

"I am going to make some plants now," the Creator said. "I will show you which ones will give you good things to eat."

Then the Creator made many kinds of trees. Among them were the hickory, the chestnut, and the oak. The Creator showed the people the nuts made by the hickory and the chestnut and the acorns made by the oak. He told them that these would be their food.

Another legend says that the Creator did not bring the people forth from the mud of the earth but rather from a great cavern that lay beneath the mound of Nanih Waiyah. At the same time that the Creator formed the people, he also made the grasshoppers, and both people and grasshoppers climbed out of the cavern together.

But then the mother of all the grasshoppers was killed by one of the people, and so no more grasshoppers came out of the cavern.

The people were also very careless of the grasshoppers, who shared the earth with them after they came out of the cavern. Sometimes the people stepped on the grasshoppers, crushing them to death. Although no more new grasshoppers were being created, ever more people were emerging from the cavern, and soon the grasshoppers became frightened that they would all be trampled to death.

"O Creator!" the grasshoppers cried. "Look at how the people trample on us! Please stop making more people, or there will be no more grasshoppers left!"

The Creator heard the grasshoppers' prayer and closed the cavern's mouth so that no more people could come out. The Creator turned the many people who were still inside the cavern into ants. This is why ants live underground but sometimes crawl out of their holes to walk around on the earth's surface.

The Building of Nanih Waiya

The sacred hill of Nanih Waiya has stood at the heart of Choctaw lands for so long that some say it was there from the time the world was made and that Nanih Waiya is the place from which the people emerged when the Creator first made the world. However, others tell a different story. They say that Nanih Waiya is a thing made by human hands and that the story of the Choctaw people begins in a land far, far away, in the west of the world.

Long ago—or so these people say—the Choctaw lived far away in the west. But their lives were uneasy because their neighbors were very warlike and gave the Choctaw no peace. The people held a council to decide what to do. In the end, the chief appointed two brothers, Chahtah and Chikasah, to lead the people to a new place where they would be safe.

That evening, the medicine man made a sacred pole and planted it in the earth in the middle of the village.

"This pole will tell us which way we should go," the medicine man said. "In the morning, we will look at the pole and go in the direction it is pointing."

In the morning, the people looked at the pole and saw that it was pointing toward the east. The people packed their belongings and began the long journey eastward. The medicine man brought the pole with him, and every night he planted it in the ground where the people were encamped. Every morning, the pole would be found leaning to the east, and so the people continued their journey eastward.

For many weeks and many months, the people walked and walked, with the pole always pointing to the east every morning. This went on until they came to the banks of a great river. None of the people had ever seen a river that wide.

"What are we to do?" they asked. "Are we to cross and continue our journey? We have never crossed a river like that before."

The medicine man said, "We will camp here tonight, and in the morning, we will see what the sacred pole tells us to do."

In the morning, the pole was pointing to the east, telling the people they must cross the river. The people made rafts and canoes. They boarded these craft with their belongings, and so crossed the great river. On the eastern bank of the river, the people resumed their journey because that is what the pole had told them to do. After a very long day's walk, they made camp, and in the morning, they looked at the pole to see where they must go next, but they found the pole was standing upright, just as the medicine man had planted it the night before.

"This means that this is the place where we are to live," the medicine man said.

To celebrate their arrival in their new home, the people built a great mound, and this is how Nanih Waiyah was made.

The people lived near Nanih Waiyah peacefully for many years, but soon the brothers, Chahtah and Chikasah, had a falling out.

"One of us needs to leave," Chahtah said.

"Yes," Chikasah said. "But how shall we decide which one?"

They went to the medicine man for help.

The medicine man said, "One of you shall stand there, and the other there. I shall place the pole between you. I will let go of the pole, and whoever the pole points to when it falls is the one who must leave."

The brothers agreed that this would be the solution, and when the pole was dropped, it pointed to Chikasah. Chikasah and his followers then packed up their belongings and moved to the north.

The Hunters and the Unknown Woman

Once two hunters had tried for two days to catch something to bring back to their families, with no success. They were now at the end of the second day, and the only thing to show for their efforts was one black hawk, which they had shot earlier that day. The hawk certainly was not enough to bring home for their families. It wasn't even really enough for the two of them, but they plucked it and set it over a fire to cook anyway since they had no other food and they were very hungry after a hard day's work.

The two men sat next to the fire waiting for their dinner to be ready. They did not speak to one another but rather sat lost in their thoughts and feeling sad about their lack of success. Just as the full moon began to rise, they heard a low, plaintive sound.

"What was that?" the first hunter asked.

"Sounded like a dove of some kind," the second replied.

"Maybe."

They sat by the fire a little longer as the moon rose into the sky. When the moon was high enough in the sky to cover everything in silvery light, the sound happened again, except this time, it was much louder and closer.

"Did you hear that? It is that sound again," the first hunter said. "It's getting closer. I think we ought to go and see what it is."

The second hunter agreed.

They went to the nearby riverbank but did not see anything along it or across it. However, when they turned around to go back to their camp, a young woman was standing on a small mound before them. She was dressed all in white clothing and very beautiful.

"Do you have anything to eat?" the woman asked the hunters. "I am very hungry indeed."

"We do not have much," the second hunter said, "but what we have, you are welcome to share."

The hunters brought the roasted hawk over to the mound and gave it to the woman. She ate some of it and gave the rest back to the hunters.

"Thank you," she said. "I was nearly dead of hunger, but you saved me. I will never forget your kindness. One month from now, return to this spot, and you will find a gift waiting for you."

Then the woman vanished, her form dissipating on the breeze.

In the morning, the hunters returned to their village, still sadly empty-handed. They did not tell anyone about the woman they had met, because they knew she was a very important and powerful being: the daughter of the Great Spirit.

The days passed, and the hunters returned to the mound on the day the woman had told them to be there. They waited and waited, but the woman did not appear. Soon it was nightfall, and the full moon was rising over the river, just as it had done on the day they had met the woman.

"I don't think she is coming," the first hunter said.

"She promised, though," the second said. "Maybe we are waiting in the wrong place. Maybe we're supposed to be waiting on the mound where we first saw her."

The hunters then went to the mound, and when they got to the top, they saw that it was covered with many tall plants. The leaves were long and flat, and growing on the stalks were long pods with silky tassels peeking out of the ends.

"What do we do with this?" the first hunter asked.

"Maybe it is something to eat. We gave her food when she was hungry, so maybe she's repaying us in kind," the second replied.

The second hunter picked one of the long pods and stripped away the leafy outer covering. He pulled off the strands of silk that lay along the rows between the kernels and took a bite.

"Oh, this is very good!" he said. "We must bring this back to the people. We can plant this, and then we will always have food right there in our village. We'll never be hungry again!"

The two hunters gathered as much corn as possible and brought it back to their village. They told the people how they had come by it. The people were all astonished and rejoiced that such a precious gift should have been given to them.

And this is how the Choctaws first got corn.

The Hunter and the Alligator

One winter, the village hunters all went out to see whether they might get some deer to bring home. All the hunters but one successfully brought down some fine deer, which they took back to their village. However, one hunter was not so lucky. He tried shooting the deer he saw, but every arrow went amiss. He wandered in the forest for three days and caught nothing to bring home.

Near the end of the third day, he decided to give up and go back to his village.

No sooner had he started his journey than he heard an strange, raspy voice say, "Please help me."

The hunter looked around but could not see anyone.

He turned back to his path home, but then the voice said, "Please, do not leave me here. I'll die. Help me."

"Where are you?" the hunter asked.

"Over here."

The hunter went toward the sound of the voice, and soon he came across an alligator. The alligator looked very ill and weak, with very dry skin.

"Please help me," the alligator said. "I need to get to water soon, or I will die. Is there any water nearby?"

"Oh, yes," the hunter replied. "There is a nice river off that way, through the forest."

"Can you carry me there? I am too weak and sick to walk all that way myself."

"No, I don't think I should do that."

"I will not eat you. I won't even bite. Not one little nibble. Just please, please carry me to the water, or I will surely die."

The hunter looked at the alligator, and although he felt very sorry for it, he still was not sure whether he could trust the animal's word. But then he hit upon an idea.

"I will carry you on one condition," the hunter said.

"Name it," the alligator said.

"You must let me tie up your feet so that your claws cannot scratch me. And you must let me tie up your mouth, so you can't bite me."

"That is fair. I promise I won't bite or scratch."

The hunter cut some vines, and with some of them, he tied the alligator's jaws tight shut. Then he tied the alligator's feet. The alligator made no protest at all; it just lay there patiently while the hunter tied it up.

"There," the hunter said. "Now, I will carry you to the river. I'll untie you when we get there. I expect you to keep your word that you won't hurt me because if you try, I'll have to kill you, and I'd rather not do that."

The alligator made a noise that the hunter took for assent and then hoisted the animal up onto his shoulders and walked to the river. At the riverbank, he gently put the alligator down and cut the bonds on its feet and mouth with his knife. True to its word, the alligator did not try to bite or scratch but rather slithered into the water. It dove beneath the surface and then came up again. It dove and surfaced three more times and then went down again and stayed down for a long time. Just as the hunter was about to turn to go home, the alligator came back up.

"Wait!" the alligator said. "You saved my life. I cannot let you leave without a gift. I see that you have been out hunting. If you do what I say, you will never return home empty-handed, and your family will always have plenty to eat. Go into the forest, and when you see a small doe, do not shoot it. Next, you will see a large doe and then a small buck, but do not shoot either of them. Last you will see a very large buck. Shoot it and bring it home to your village."

Then the alligator slid back into the water, and the hunter never saw it again.

The hunter started on his journey back home, hunting as he went. He saw a small doe, but he did not shoot it. Then he saw a large doe, but he did not shoot it either. Not long afterward, he saw a small buck, but he let that one go too. Finally, he came across a large buck. He nocked an arrow to the string and took a shot. The deer went down, killed instantly. The hunter brought the buck home, and from that day forward, he never returned to his village empty-handed, and his family always had plenty to eat.

The Boys Who Followed the Sun

Once there were twin brothers named Tashka and Walo. They were very curious about the world around them and always wanted to know more. When they were about four years old, they began to watch the Sun as it rose in the east, moved across the sky, and set in the west.

They went to their mother and said, "Mother, where does the Sun go at night?"

"Nobody knows," their mother replied. "I was always told that the Sun dies when it sets and is born again when it rises in the morning."

Soon the boys could talk of nothing other than where the Sun went every night. They asked many people, but none gave the boys a satisfactory answer.

One day, Tashka and Walo watched the Sun rise and move across the sky, as they had been doing for some time, but when it set that night, they said to one another, "Let us follow the Sun. We will see for ourselves where it goes at night."

Off they went, even though they were only four years old.

For many days, they followed the Sun through country they knew very well, but still, they came no closer to the place where the Sun went to die. They kept traveling through country they did not know at all, but even though they traveled very far every day, they still came no closer to the Sun's home.

The boys traveled day after day, year after year until they were grown into young men.

Finally, they came to the edge of the land. Before them was a wide sea, so broad that they could not see what lay on the other side.

They sat on the beach to watch the Sun set, and as it did, Tashka said, "I bet the Sun lives over the edge of the sea. If we go there, we will be at his house."

"Yes," Walo said. "We should journey across the sea, too, and if we get to the edge when the Sun does, we can follow him home."

The next morning, the boys built themselves a sturdy canoe, and in the evening, they began paddling across the water.

They arrived at the edge of the sea just as the Sun did, so the boys could follow the Sun into his home.

In the Sun's home, there was a multitude of women. Most of the women were stars, but one woman was the Moon, and she was the Sun's wife.

The Moon saw the boys and said, "How did you come here? Mortal beings do not belong in this house."

"We are Tashka and Walo," the boys said. "We wanted to know where the Sun goes every night. We have been following him, day after day, year after year since we were tiny children."

Then the Sun saw the boys. He said to his wife, "Go and boil a big pot of water."

The Moon did as she was bid, and when the water was boiling, the Sun put the boys into the pot. When they had been in the water a little while, the Sun reached in and rubbed their bodies until their skin came off, and they were red all over.

When the boiling was done, the Sun said, "Now, tell me why you are here. You are still living men, and it is not time for you to join me here in my house."

The boys explained that they had followed him, day after day, year after year because they wanted to see where he died at night.

"That was bravely done," the Sun said, "but you can't stay. I have to send you home now. But listen to me: Once you reach your home, you may not speak to anyone for four days. If you speak before the four days are over, you will die soon thereafter. If you speak after the four days are over, then you will have long and happy lives."

The Sun then summoned Buzzard. He put Tashka and Walo on Buzzard's back and told him to take the young men home. Buzzard flew up into the sky and wheeled around until he found the right direction to go. Down and down he flew, until he reached the clouds. This part of the journey was easy because above the clouds, there is never any wind. But once Buzzard got below the clouds, a strong wind began to blow him to and fro.

"Hang on tight!" Buzzard said to the young men as he tried to keep them safely on his back.

No matter how hard the wind blew, Buzzard kept flying toward Tashka and Walo's home, and soon the young men were safely on the ground not far from their village. Tashka and Walo bid Buzzard farewell and walked a little way down the path, but they were so shaken from their dangerous flight that they decided to rest awhile under a tree.

While the young men were resting, a man from their village passed by. He saw Tashka and Walo and greeted them, but they did not reply.

"Why won't you speak to me? Are you ill? Have I offended you?" the man asked.

But no matter what the man said, the young men would not answer.

"Oh, well. You don't have to talk if you don't want to, but someone has to tell your mother that you are back. She has been mourning you all these long years and will be so happy to see you again."

Soon Tashka and Walo's mother came running up the path, weeping with joy. She embraced her children and noted what fine young men they had become.

"Where have you been? We looked everywhere for you, for so very long. I missed you terribly, and I am so happy to see you alive again," she said.

The boys did not answer her, for they meant to follow the Sun's instructions. Their mother kept asking question after question, but when the boys remained silent, she became angry. Finally, she forced them to speak.

"We went to see where the Sun dies at night," the young men said. "We journeyed day after day, year after year until we came to the Sun's house. He put us on a buzzard that carried us home, but he also said that we would die soon thereafter if we spoke before four days had passed after our arrival home. That is why we were not answering you."

At this, the mother became very sorrowful. "I should not have forced you to speak. I am sorry for that. But come home now and have a meal, and tell me where you have been and what you have seen."

The young men went home with their mother. She cooked them a fine meal, and they told the story of their adventures to all the village. When their tale was ended, they both lay down on the ground and died. It was then that they went back to the Sun's house, where they have lived ever since.

The Owl Woman

Some children were playing outside their house when they saw someone coming down the path toward their village.

"Who is that?" one child asked.

"I don't know. I've never seen someone like that before," another replied.

"Let's go and see who it is!" a third said, and so off they went to greet the stranger.

However, the children had not gone far when they saw that the stranger was a very old woman. Her body was bent with age, and her hair was white. In her hands, she carried a basket with a lid. She was so old and so bent that the children became frightened and ran back home. But soon, curiosity overcame them, and they went out to greet the old woman, who had arrived in their village at that time.

"Don't be afraid of me," the woman said. "After all, I am your great-great-great-grandmother! You have never seen me because I live very far away. Even your mother has never seen me! But maybe you can go and fetch your mother, and tell her that I have come to visit."

The children did as the old woman bid them, and soon their mother had helped the old woman into the house and given her a deerskin to sit on. The mother and her children prepared a meal and gave it to the woman.

When the woman was done eating, she asked the children, "Tell me about your father. When he is home, where does he sleep?"

The children pointed out the place where their father slept.

That night, when the family was asleep, the old woman went to the place where the father lay and cut off his head. She put the head in her basket and covered the body with a blanket. Then she crept silently out of the house.

In the morning, the mother woke and started about the business of the day. She saw that her husband was still in bed, which was strange because he usually was the first one up.

"Are you ill, husband? Why are you still in bed?" she asked.

When her husband did not answer, the wife pulled off the blanket. She was horrified to find her husband's headless body beneath it.

Meanwhile, the old woman was hastening down the path away from the village, carrying the basket with the man's head in it. After a time, she came across a bear.

"Good morning," the bear said. "What do you have in your basket?"

"Oh, it is something very dangerous indeed. If I show it to you, you will instantly become blind. That's how bad it is," she replied.

The bear was alarmed by this and asked no further questions and went on his way.

The woman continued down the road until she met a deer. The deer also asked what was in the basket, and when the woman warned him that he would go blind if he saw it, the deer asked no further questions and went on his way.

All throughout the day, the woman met animals along the path. They all asked the same question, and she gave them all the same answer. The animals all left the woman alone after she answered them until she came across two wildcats.

"Good day, old woman," the wildcats said. "That's a fine basket you have there. Can we see inside it?"

"Oh, no. I can't show this to anyone. Whoever sees what I have in this basket will go blind instantly," she replied.

"That doesn't matter to us at all," the first wildcat said as he tore the basket out of the woman's hands and lifted the lid.

When the wildcat saw what was inside the basket, he showed it to his friend. Both wildcats were horrified and angered by what they saw.

"We've heard of you, old woman," the first wildcat said.

"Yes, indeed we have," the second said. "You killed some of our friends. Now we shall avenge them."

Then the wildcats leaped at the old woman and took her captive.

While the first wildcat held the old woman, the second went looking for something to use as a weapon to kill her with.

Once the second wildcat was out of earshot, the old woman said to the first, "You know, if you really want to kill me, you should use that tree branch over there. It looks quite solid and probably would make a fine club. Also, it is good luck to kill me. Why wait for your friend to come back and let him have all the luck? You should do it yourself. I think you deserve it more, anyway."

The first wildcat wanted that good luck for himself, so he let the woman go and went to pick up the tree branch. However, when he returned, the woman was gone, for she had turned into an owl and flown far away.

The Hunter Who Became a Deer

A hunter went out early one morning to see whether he might get any game. He spent all day in the forest, but game was scarce, and even when he did spy something, his arrows went astray. As the sun was setting, he came across a beautiful doe. He nocked an arrow to the string and let fly. The arrow found its mark, and the doe collapsed to the ground, dead.

The hunter saw that it was nearly dark, and since he was far from home, he decided to spend the night there and take the carcass home in the morning. When the sun rose, the hunter heard a voice speaking to him.

"Wake up," the voice said.

The hunter sat up, startled. He looked around, and there was the doe he had shot the night before. She was still lying on the ground, but her head was up, and she was looking right at him.

"Don't be afraid," the doe said. "I only want to ask you something. Will you come home with me?"

All the hunter could do was blink in astonishment, so the doe said, "Please come home with me."

The hunter agreed, so the doe got to her feet and began to lead the hunter through the forest.

They traveled a very long way, and soon they were in country that was unfamiliar to the hunter. Finally, they arrived at a place where there was a very large boulder. Underneath the boulder was a hole, and the doe went into it. The hunter followed her, and there before him stood the king of the deer, a huge buck with enormous antlers.

"Welcome. You have traveled a long way. You may rest if you wish," the buck said.

The hunter did not know what to say in reply, so he lay down in the place the buck showed to him and fell fast asleep.

Now, in the cave where the king of the deer lived, there were many piles of deer hooves, antlers, and skins. The buck and the doe selected various hooves and tried to fit them over the man's hands and feet, but it was some time before they found pairs that fit him perfectly. Next, they found a skin and wrapped it around his body. They finished their work by affixing a set of antlers to his head. The hunter slept soundly through all of this, and when he woke, he found that he had been turned into a deer.

He left the cave and went through the forest in deer form, and for a time, lived in the way that deer do.

When the hunter did not return home, his mother became worried. After several days had passed, she asked the village men to help her find her son. She went out with a search party, and after some time, they came across the hunter's bow and arrows, which he had left behind in the place where he had shot the doe. The people gathered around the bow and arrows and began singing together. Before they could finish the song, a herd of deer came bounding through the forest and encircled them. One buck left the circle and walked up to the hunter's mother.

"Hello, Mother. It is I, your son. The king of the deer turned me into a buck. I live with the deer now," the buck said.

All were astonished to hear the deer speak, for it spoke with the voice of the missing hunter. The mother cried out when she heard her son's voice.

"No, no! My son cannot be a deer. Take that deerskin off him," she said to the men of the search party. "I don't want to have a deer for a son. Take off the skin and the hooves and the antlers."

"Wait! Please don't remove my skin. I have become a deer, and if you do what you suggest, I will surely die," the buck said.

"No matter. I will not have a deer for a son. I'd rather you were dead," the hunter's mother said.

At that, the men grabbed the buck and began flaying off its skin, but what the buck had said was true; he had become a deer indeed, and so he died at the hands of the men from his village.

When the buck was dead, the men carried it back to the village, where the hunter's mother told everyone what had happened. Then the people buried the deer with great care, holding a sacred dance as part of the ceremony.

Part II: Legends from Other Southern Tribes

How Alligator's Nose Was Broken (*Seminole*)

One day, the animals decided to challenge the birds to a ball game. The birds agreed. Alligator was the captain of the animals' team, and Eagle was the captain of the birds' team. They found a good place to have the game and set up goalposts at either end. The medicine men for each team cast spells on the ball, hoping that this would help their team win.

Finally, it was time for the game to start. Each team gathered under its goalpost, while animals and birds for miles around stood around the perimeter of the field to watch the action. The game began when the ball was tossed into the air.

Alligator got there first and snatched up the ball in his strong jaws. He started running directly for the goal. He was so fast and so strong that none of the birds could take the ball away from him. Alligator's wife jumped up and down on the sidelines, cheering for her husband.

"That is my son's father!" she shouted. "He is the fastest and the strongest! Look at him go!"

Just as Alligator was nearing the goal, Eagle swooped down from high above the field. He swooped down so hard and so fast that when he hit Alligator in the nose, Alligator yelped with pain and almost dropped the ball. When Alligator opened his mouth to yell, Turkey ran in and, paying no mind to Alligator's sharp teeth, snatched up the ball and ran toward his goalposts. He got there before any of the animals could catch him and tossed the ball between the posts, winning the game for the birds.

And this is why the alligator has a big dent in the middle of his nose—because of the time that the eagle landed on it in a ballgame.

Rabbit and Wildcat *(Natchez)*

As Rabbit hopped down the path one morning, he saw a wildcat approaching from the other direction. Rabbit looked this way and that, wondering whether he should run away, but it was too late: Wildcat had already seen him.

"Good morning, Wildcat. I hope you had a fine breakfast before you set off down this path," Rabbit said.

Wildcat replied, "Well, no. As a matter of fact, I haven't eaten all day." He stared pointedly at Rabbit and licked his chops.

"Oh, dear. That's bad. One shouldn't start one's day without breakfast," Rabbit said.

"No, indeed."

"I think turkey makes an excellent breakfast, don't you?"

"It certainly does, but where are you going to get turkey hereabouts?"

"I know where there's a flock of the fattest turkeys you've ever seen," Rabbit said, "and I also know an easy way for you to catch one for your meal. All you have to do is lie down here in the path and pretend to be dead. I'll bring the turkeys to you. You won't have to do a thing except lie there with your mouth open, and when a turkey gets close enough, you bite, and there is your breakfast!"

"Very well. But if you're tricking me, I'll have rabbit for breakfast instead," Wildcat said.

"No, no, it's no trick. Now hold still. I need to make you look like you're actually dead."

Rabbit got some crumbs of rotten wood and put them all over Wildcat's face to make it look like the flies had already been there and laid their eggs on his carcass.

"There. Now you look really dead. Hold still. I'm going to get the turkeys now," Rabbit said.

Rabbit hopped down the path until he came to the place where the turkeys were scratching for grubs.

"Hey, turkeys!" Rabbit shouted. "Have I got some good news for you! You know that wildcat that keeps eating you all the time? Well, he's dead! He's dead, and his body is just up the path there. Let's all go and have a dance to celebrate. You can dance around him, and I'll sing for you."

The turkeys whooped for joy and gladly followed Rabbit down the path.

There Wildcat lay, not moving a muscle.

"He really is dead!" one of the turkeys said.

"Yes, he really is!" Rabbit said. "Now, how about that dance?"

Then Rabbit began to sing:

Catch that big old turkey!

Catch the one with the red head!

Catch the one with the big tail!

"Hang on a minute," the turkeys said. "Are you sure that's the right song?"

"Very sure. I mean, Wildcat is dead, and he can't hurt you, right? I think it's the perfect song for the occasion," Rabbit replied.

Rabbit kept singing as the turkeys danced round and round Wildcat.

Sometimes Rabbit would say, "Now how about you jump on him? He can't hurt you! It'll be fun!" and the turkeys would jump on Wildcat's body.

Wildcat lay ever so still throughout all of this until, finally, one turkey came just a little too close to Wildcat's open jaws.

Snap!

Wildcat's sharp teeth closed over the turkey's neck, and all the rest of the birds flew away in fright.

Wildcat stood up and looked around for Rabbit, but Rabbit was nowhere to be seen. As soon as Wildcat had caught his meal, Rabbit had run away just as the turkeys had done, and so managed to live another day.

The Sky Maidens' Canoe (*Alabama*)

There once was an Alabama village close to a river. The people were accustomed to seeing canoes being paddled up and down the river by people going fishing or visiting relatives in another village, or taking items to trade elsewhere.

One day, something happened that they had never seen before: a canoe came floating down from the sky instead of down the river. The canoe was full of young women, and when they had beached their craft on the riverbank, they all got out and began to play a game of ball. The people of the village watched in astonishment, not knowing what to say or do. After a time, the young women tired of their game. They got back in their canoe and pushed it out into the water, but instead of floating down the river, it floated back up into the sky.

Now, seeing a canoe full of young women come down from the sky is wondrous enough when it happens once, but the young women kept coming back. For several days, they floated down in their canoe, played a game of ball, and then went back home up into the sky. One of the young men of the village watched the young women the entire time they were there, and soon he fell in love with one of them and decided that he must have her for his wife.

The next time the sky maidens arrived in their canoe, the young man hid in some bushes near the place where the young women played ball, and when the one he desired got close enough, he jumped out of the bushes and grabbed her. When the other maidens saw what had happened to their companion, they ran back to their canoe in fright. They sailed back up into the sky, leaving their friend behind.

"Don't be afraid," the young man said to the maiden he had captured. "I'm not going to hurt you. I love you, and I want you to be my wife."

And so, the young man married the sky maiden, and in time, they had several children together. The young man made a large canoe to hold his growing family and a smaller one to use when he went hunting.

One day, the children said to their father, "We are so very hungry. Can you go hunting for us? Bring us back a fine, fat deer to eat."

The man went out hunting, but he returned without having caught anything.

The next day, the children again asked their father to go hunting and bring home a deer, and again the man went out into the forest. This time, as soon as the father had gone, the sky woman gathered all her children and put them into the large canoe. She got into the canoe next to her children and began to sing her magic song, which made the canoe rise into the air. The father heard the song and recognized it. He rushed home and grabbed the canoe, pulling it back down to earth.

When the father went out hunting again, the sky woman put all her children into the large canoe and then got into the small one herself. She began to sing her magic song, and the canoes began to rise into the sky. The hunter again heard the song and ran home, but this time, he could only catch the canoe that had the children in it. The one with the sky woman continued floating up into the air until it was lost from sight.

Many days passed. The children often cried for their mother, and the father missed his wife.

Finally, he asked his children, "Can you sing the sky song your mother sang?"

"Yes, we can," the children replied.

"Good. In the morning, we will all get into the large canoe. We will sing the sky song, and hopefully, it will take us up to the place where your mother is."

When the sun rose, the man and his children got into the large canoe. They sang the sky song, and the canoe began to float up into the air. The canoe rose up and up until, finally, it came to the land above the clouds.

The man and his children got out of the canoe. They began to walk toward a nearby house, where an old woman sat just outside the door.

"Welcome," the old woman said. "Why have you come here?"

"My wife is here and has been here for many days. My children miss their mother and would like to see her again," the man said.

"Yes, you may see her again. She is just over there. She spends her days singing and dancing. But you have had a long journey and should eat before you go to her. Please, sit down, and I will bring you a meal."

The man and his children sat down, and soon the old woman brought out a single cooked squash.

"I don't think that's going to be enough for all of us," the man said.

"Never fear. There's always plenty when I make a meal."

The man and his children ate the squash, but they were still hungry. Lo and behold, another cooked squash appeared in the place of the one they had eaten! The man and his children ate that squash, too, and another, and another until they were so full they could not eat another bite. After the squash was all gone, the old woman brought the family some corn, but they did not eat it. Instead, they went to look for the sky woman and took some of the corn with them.

They walked until they came across another house.

The man asked the person who lived in the house, "Where is my wife and my children's mother?"

"She is just over there. She is singing and dancing," the person replied.

No sooner had the person said that than the sky woman came dancing past, but she did not recognize her husband and children. The next time she danced past, the children took some of the corn and tossed it at her, but although she still paid them no mind, she did smell the scent of the corn.

I know that scent, she thought. *That's like the corn I used to eat when I was on earth.*

The third time she danced past, the children tossed corn at her again, and this time, she noticed them. She ran to her husband and children and embraced them with great joy. Together the family got into their canoes and went back down to their home near the river.

For a time, the sky woman was happy living with her husband and children, but she missed her sky home very much.

Finally, she went to her husband and said, "I love you, my husband, but I cannot stay here. The sky is my home. My children and I belong there. Tomorrow we will be going back, and we shall not return."

The husband was very sad, but he knew it would be wrong to force his wife and children to stay. In the morning, they said tearful goodbyes to one another. Then the woman and her children got into the large canoe, which floated back up into the sky when the woman sang her magic song.

For a long time, the man was sad because he missed his wife and children. However, eventually, he married another woman from his own people, and they lived happily together for many years.

The King of the Tie-Snakes (*Creek*)

One day, a village chief summoned his son to him.

The chief handed the boy a beautiful clay bowl and said, "My son, take this to the chief of the village to the north, and give him a message that I will tell to you. The bowl will show the chief that you are my son, and you speak for me."

The chief told his son the message, and the boy left on his errand.

On the way, the boy came to the banks of a river, where some other children were throwing stones into the water. Wanting to join in the fun and not thinking about what he was doing, the boy threw the bowl his father had given him into the water, where it promptly sank.

Oh, no! the boy thought. *I can't complete my errand without that bowl, and I surely can't tell my father what I just did. What shall I do?*

After a moment's thought, the boy decided to dive into the water to see whether he might find the bowl. The water was very deep; the boy swam down and down and down without reaching the bottom, and the further down he went, the darker it got.

Finally, he reached the riverbed and began feeling around with his hands, trying to find the bowl. He had not searched for long when he felt his arms and legs enwrapped by writhing, slimy creatures. He had been captured by tie-snakes!

The tie-snakes brought the boy to an underwater cave. In the cave was a tall dais, and at the top sat the king of the tie-snakes.

"Climb up to the top," the tie-snakes said to the boy.

The boy put his foot onto the base of the dais but recoiled when he found that it was made of a mass of writhing tie-snakes.

"Come on, climb up to the top!" the tie-snakes repeated, so the boy tried again.

It was very difficult to find places to put his hands and feet, and the surface of the dais kept shifting with the writhing of the snakes, but finally, he made it to the top.

"Come and sit near me," the king of the tie-snakes said. When the boy was seated, the king added, "Look over there. There's a beautiful feather hanging from the roof of my cave. It's yours if you can hold onto it."

The boy went over to the feather and put his hand around it, but it slid out of his grasp. He tried again, and again the feather slipped away. The boy kept trying, and on the fourth attempt, he held onto the feather.

The king of the tie-snakes pointed to a tomahawk in another corner of the cave. "You can have that, too, if you can hold onto it."

The boy went to the tomahawk and tried to get hold of it, but it slipped out of his grasp. He kept trying, and on the fourth attempt, he was able to hold onto the tomahawk.

The king then said to the boy, "You must be my guest for three days. After that time, you can go back home, but on no account must you tell your father where you have been or what you have seen. When he asks you, you must say, 'I know what I know,' and nothing else. But if your father needs my help, you may tell him that you know how to get that help for him, and this is what you shall do: At dawn, walk eastward with the feather and tomahawk and bow three times toward the rising sun. When you do that, I will send aid to your father."

The boy spent three days among the tie-snakes, and on the third day, they brought him back to the place where he had dived into the water. The tie-snakes gave him back the bowl, which he carried along with the feather and the tomahawk from the tie-snakes' cave. The boy swam back to dry land and ran home to his father, who had given his son up for dead.

"Where have you been? We all thought you had drowned in the river," the chief said.

"I know what I know, but if ever you need help, the king of the tie-snakes has offered his assistance to you," the boy replied.

For many days, the chief and his son lived peacefully among their people, but there came a time when a messenger arrived saying that a neighboring chief was planning an attack on the village.

The chief said to his son, "I think now is a good time to ask the king of the tie-snakes for help."

"I will go at sunrise. That is what I was told to do," the boy said.

In the morning, the boy took the feather and the tomahawk and walked eastward. He bowed three times to the rising sun, and when he stood up after his third bow, there was the king of the tie-snakes.

"You have summoned me. What may I do to help you?" the king of the tie-snakes asked.

"Another chief is preparing to attack our village. Can you help us defeat our enemies?"

"Yes. Tell your father that all will be arranged and that he will be victorious," the king of the tie-snakes replied.

The boy went home and told his father what the king of the tie-snakes had said.

That night, the enemy chief and his warriors launched an attack on the village, but they did not get far. The chief and his people didn't even know there had been an attack until they went outside and saw the enemy warriors lying on the ground, all tied up by tie-snakes.

The chief of the village and his men took the enemy's chief and warriors prisoner. The two chiefs talked together and made peace, so the tie-snakes let the other warriors go to their homes unharmed and slithered back to their home under the river.

The Owl Bridegroom (*Caddo*)

Once there were twin girls whose ambition was to marry a powerful chief. They always kept their ears open for news, and soon they heard that a powerful chief lived nearby and that he was unmarried.

The girls went to their parents and said, "We want to go to the village of that powerful, wealthy chief and see whether he will take us as wives. May we go?"

The parents gave their blessing, so the girls set out on the road to find the village they had heard about.

They had traveled some way when the first girl said, "I wonder how far it is to that village. We have been walking for a long time and have not seen anyone."

"Yes," the second girl said. "Maybe we should ask for directions. Let's keep going this way, and if we come across anyone, we will ask."

The first girl agreed that this was a good idea, and so the two girls resumed their journey. It wasn't long before they saw a man carrying a turkey in one hand walking down the path toward them.

The girls greeted him and said, "We're looking for the village of a powerful and wealthy chief. We want to be his wives. Would you happen to know where that village is?"

Of course, the man had no idea what village they were talking about, but they were both beautiful girls, so he wanted them to be his wives.

"Well, today you are in luck! I just so happen to be that chief. I'm here on the road because I've just been to a big council. Very important. It's the kind of thing I do—I'm powerful, and all the other chiefs respect me. I would certainly like to have you both for my wives, but first, I need to go home and consult with my grandmother," the man said.

The girls thought it odd that a powerful chief would need to ask his grandmother's permission to marry, but they agreed to wait until he returned.

Now, this man was no chief. He was simply Owl.

He ran home and told his grandmother, "We need to clean the house, quickly! I have met two beautiful girls who think I am a powerful chief, so they want to marry me. If we do things right, we can fool them."

Owl and his grandmother put the house to rights, and then Owl hung the turkey he had caught from the rafters.

"Here is what we will do with the turkey. In the morning, ask them which turkey you should cook for us to eat. Pretend to point to one in a different part of the house. I'll tell you to cook this one that I just hung up. It will make the girls think that we always have plenty of food," the man said.

Owl went back to the place where the girls were waiting and took them back to his home. He introduced them to his grandmother, and when the girls saw how nicely the home was kept, they agreed to marry Owl and live with him.

Now, every day afterward, Owl came home with a turkey, which he claimed to have hunted. But this wasn't true; in fact, he was going to the council of a powerful chief every day. The chief sat on Owl's back during the council and paid Owl for his trouble by giving him a turkey.

After a time, the girls began to tire of eating nothing but turkey.

"I wonder whether our husband really does go hunting every day," the first girl said.

"Yes, it does seem strange that he never brings home anything but turkey. Let's follow him tomorrow and see where he really goes," the second girl said.

In the morning, Owl left the house and headed for the council place as he usually did, and the girls followed behind him as stealthily as they could. They waited in some bushes when Owl went into the council house, and when they thought it was safe, the girls crept up to the door and peeked through the crack. There they saw their husband, with the powerful chief sitting on his back! The two girls were so shocked they screamed.

Owl recognized his wives' voices and stood up in alarm, throwing the chief down to the ground. Owl then ran home and shouted at his grandmother for letting the girls out of her sight.

For their part, the girls felt ashamed at having been fooled so badly, so they returned to their parents' home, where they told their mother and father everything that had happened.

Kutnahin's Gifts

A time came when a group of young men decided to see whether they could walk to the place where the sky meets the earth.

"Maybe we can even get into the sky country!" one man said.

"Yes! I've always wondered what the sky country is like," another said.

So, the men set out on their journey. They walked to the north for many, many days until finally, they reached the place where the sky meets the earth. There they found the sky rising and falling. Each time it rose, a path to the sky country was opened, but when it fell, it came down very, very fast. The young men decided that it was worth the risk to run under the sky when it opened. They waited until the time was right and then ran as fast as they could through the gap. Unfortunately, only six of the men were fast enough to get all the way through; the others were crushed when the sky fell back down.

The men traveled through the sky country until they came to the home of Kutnahin.

"Welcome. You can stay here as long as you like," Kutnahin said to the men.

After many days in the sky country, the men decided that they wanted to go back home.

Kutnahin asked them, "In what form would you like to return to earth?"

"I'd like to be a squirrel, please," the first man said, so Kutnahin changed him into a squirrel.

The man tried to jump from the sky down to the earth, but it was too far a distance. When he hit the earth, he died.

Kutnahin asked the next man what form he would like to assume. That man also chose an animal form and died when he plummeted from the sky to the earth.

Another man tried his luck as an animal, and he also died.

When Kutnahin asked the fourth man what he would like to become, the man said, "Change me into a spider."

Kutnahin granted his request, and so the man attached one end of his silk line to the sky and carefully lowered himself down to the earth.

The fifth man asked to be made an eagle. He spread his wings and glided down from the sky.

The sixth man said he wanted to be a pigeon. He also flew down safely to earth.

Now, not only had Kutnahin changed the forms of these men, but he had also given them special gifts to share. To the man who became a spider, he gave knowledge of healing songs and dances. This man became the first healer, and he taught what he knew to the people of his tribe. But a sorrowful thing had happened while that man was visiting Kutnahin. One of the people of his village died before the spider came back down to earth, so the spider could not heal him. This is how death came to the world.

The man who came back as an eagle showed the people how to catch fish, and the man who came back as a pigeon showed the people how to grow corn. The gifts of these men meant that the people would always have good things to eat.

The Girl and the Panther (*Creek*)

In a village near a river lived four brothers and their little sister. Not far from their village lived Istepapa, the panther, whose name means "man-eater."

One day, Istepapa was paddling his canoe down the river and happened to pass by the girl's village. There, he saw the girl, who was drawing water from the river.

Istepapa guided his boat to the riverbank and called to the girl, "Come and take a ride in my canoe!"

"Oh, no, I mustn't. I've heard stories about men like you. I won't get into your canoe," the girl replied.

"All right. But what if I told you I have a basket full of panther cubs here? Would you like to see them?"

The girl hesitated, but she did love baby animals, so she got into the canoe. No sooner had she sat down than Istepapa pushed off from the riverbank and paddled down the river as fast as he could toward his home. The girl screamed for help, but all her brothers were out hunting, and the other people of the village were too far away to hear her.

When Istepapa got home with the girl, he gave her to his wife and said, "Here. Look after this girl. See that she does not run away."

In the morning, Istepapa got ready to go out hunting. He said to his wife and the girl, "I expect you to be ready to cook dinner as soon as I get home. Make me soup from acorns and meat. Find the acorns and wash them well in the stream."

Then Istepapa left the house.

The wife said to the girl, "Oh, it is most unfortunate that you are here. You should know that if my husband comes back without any game, he takes a chunk of my flesh to eat. I'm sure he'll do the same to you if you don't get away."

"How can I escape?" the girl asked. "I don't even know where I am or how to get back to my village."

"I will help you. But first, we'll gather some acorns. Then we'll ask Kotee the frog to help us."

The girl and the woman gathered acorns and went to the riverbank. There, they found Kotee.

"This girl is in trouble. Will you help her?" Istepapa's wife said to the frog.

"Yes, indeed I will. What must I do?" Kotee replied.

"Take these acorns. When Istepapa returns, he will ask whether the acorns have been washed. You must tell him no."

"Very well. I will do that."

Then the wife turned to the girl. "It's time for you to go. Run away as fast as you can. Follow the river upstream, and you should come to your village. Always run! Istepapa surely will come after you, and you need to get home before he catches you."

The girl thanked the wife and then ran off up the riverbank as she had been told to do.

When Istepapa got home, he said, "Little girl, did you wash my acorns?"

Kotee replied from the riverbank, "No."

Istepapa was puzzled. He heard the voice, but couldn't see the girl.

So again, he asked, "Little girl, did you wash my acorns?"

And again, Kotee replied, "No."

Istepapa went down to the riverbank—since that is where the voice seemed to be coming from. Seeing Istepapa approach, Kotee jumped into the water with a splash.

"Aha! You can't get away from me that way!" Istepapa said.

He dove into the water where he had heard the splash, thinking that the girl was trying to escape by swimming. Istepapa dove down under the water, but he could not see the girl anywhere. He surfaced and looked up and down the river but still did not find the girl.

Istepapa went back home and took out his magic wheel that could find anything he told it to find. Istepapa threw the wheel in one direction, but it came right back. He tried another direction and another, but each time the wheel returned. Finally, he tried the direction in which the girl's village lay, and the wheel did not come back.

Istepapa followed the wheel, and soon he began catching up to the girl.

He could hear her voice singing as she ran:

I have to reach my brothers' house before they catch me.

I have to reach my brothers' house before they catch me.

Now, the girl had nearly reached her brothers' house, and her youngest brother heard her song.

He went to his elder brothers and said, "I hear our sister's voice. I think she's in danger. Let's go help her."

The brothers all went out of the house and stood listening. The sound of their sister's song was even closer now.

They heard her singing:

I have to reach my brothers' house before they catch me.

I have to reach my brothers' house before they catch me.

"Yes, that is our sister," the elder brothers said to the youngest. "We're going to go help her, but you stay here. You're too young for this task."

"I am not too young. I'm coming, too, and you can't stop me," the youngest brother said.

The four brothers ran toward their sister's voice.

Soon they saw their sister running toward them, and not far behind her were the wheel and Istepapa. The girl ran past them and straight into their house. The elder brothers all shot arrows at the wheel and Istepapa, but they missed. Then the youngest brother took the paddle that he used for preparing food. He ran up to the wheel and smashed it with the paddle. Then he ran up to Istepapa and struck him a great blow on his head, killing him instantly.

"It's a good thing you came with us. We all surely would have died but for you, and you saved our sister," the elder brothers said.

Bibliography

Brown, Virginia Pounds, and Laurella Owens, eds. *Southern Indian Myths and Legends.* Birmingham: Beechwood Books, 1985.

Bushnell, David I., Jr. *Native Ceremonies and Forms of Burial East of the Mississippi.* Washington, DC: Government Printing Office, 1920.

———. "Myths of the Louisiana Choctaw." *American Anthropologist* n.s. 12/4 (1910): 526–35.

———. *The Choctaw of Bayou Lacomb, St. Tammany Parish.* Washington, D.C.: Government Printing Office, 1909.

Curry, Jane Louise. *The Wonderful Sky Boat and Other Native American Tales of the Southeast.* New York: Margaret K. McElderry Books, 2001.

Dorsey, George Amos. *Traditions of the Caddo.* Washington, D.C.: Carnegie Institute, 1905.

Eastman, Elaine Goodale. *Indian Legends Retold.* Boston: Little, Brown, and Company, 1919.

Grantham, Bill. *Creation Myths and Legends of the Creek Indians.* Gainesville: University Press of Florida, 2002

Lankford, George E. *Native American Legends: Southeastern Legends—Tales From the Natchez, Caddo, Biloxi, Chicasaw, and Other Nations.* Little Rock: August House, 1987.

Macfarlan, Allan A., ed. *Native American Tales and Legends.* Mineola: Dover Publications, Inc., 1968.

McKee, Jesse O., and Jon A. Schlenker. *The Choctaws: Cultural Evolution of a Native American Tribe.* Jackson: University Press of Mississippi, 1980.

McNeese, Tim. *Illustrated Myths of Native America: The Northeast, Southeast, Great Lakes and Great Plains.* London: Blandford, 1998.

Peterson, John H., Jr., ed. *A Choctaw Source Book.* New York: Garland Publishing, Inc., 1985.

Swanton, John R. *Source Material for the Social and Ceremonial Life of the Choctaw Indians.* Washington, D.C.: Government Printing Office, 1931.

——. "Animal Stories From the Indians of the Muskohegan Stock." *Journal of American Folk-Lore* 26 (1913): 193-218.

——. "Mythology of the Indians of Louisiana and the Texas Coast." *Journal of American Folk-Lore* 20 (1907): 285-89.

Thompson, Stith. *Tales of the North American Indians.* Cambridge, MA: Harvard University Press, 1929.

Bastian, Dawn Elaine, and Judy K. Mitchell. *Handbook of Native American Mythology.* Santa Barbara: ABC-CLIO, 2004.

Berk, Ari, and Carolyn Dunn. *Coyote Speaks: Wonders of the Native American World.* New York: Harry N. Abrams, Inc., 2008.

Brown, Virginia Pounds, and Laurella Owens. *Southern Indian Myths and Legends.* Birmingham: Beechwood Books, 1985.

Cherokee Nation, "History." Accessed 21 September 2020. https://www.cherokee.org/about-the-nation/history/.

Dale, Edward Everett. *Tales of the Tepee.* Boston: D. C. Heath & Co., [1920].

Judson, Katharine B. *Native American Legends of the Great Lakes and Mississippi Valley.* Dekalb: Northern Illinois University Press, 2000.

Lankford, George, ed. *Native American Legends: Southeastern Legends: Tales from the Natchez, Caddo, Biloxi, Chickasaw, and Other Nations.* Little Rock: August House, 1987.

Mooney, James. *Myths of the Cherokee.* Washington, DC: Government Printing Office, 1902.

Morris, Cora. *Stories from Mythology: North American.* Boston: Marshall Jones Company, 1924.

Pijoan, Teresa. *White Wolf Woman: Native American Transformation Myths.* Little Rock: August House Publishers, Inc., 1992.

Taylor, Colin, ed. *Native American Myths and Legends.* London: Salamander Books, Ltd., 1994.

Young, Richard, and Judy Dockrey, eds. *Race with Buffalo and Other Native American Stories for Young Readers.* Little Rock: August House Publishers, Inc., 1994.

Albert, Roy, et al. *Coyote Tales (English Version)*. Flagstaff: North Arizona Supplementary Education Center, 1970.

Arkansas Archeological Survey. "Story 4: Coyote and the Origins of Death." *Indians of Arkansas.* <archeology.uark.edu/indiansofarkansas/index.html?pageName=Story 4: Coyote and the Origins of Death> Accessed 9 August 2019.

Barrett, Samuel Alfred. "Pomo Myths." *Bulletin of the Public Museum of the City of Milwaukee* 15 (1933): 1-608.

———. *Myths of the Southern Sierra Miwok*. Berkeley: University of California Press, 1919.

Bayliss, Clara K. *A Treasury of Eskimo Tales*. New York: Thomas Y. Crowell Company, 1922.

Bierhorst, John. *The Mythology of North America*. New York: William Morrow and Company, 1985.

Bloomfield, Leonard. *Menomini Texts*. New York: G. E. Stechert, 1928.

Clark, Ella E. *Indian Legends of the Pacific Northwest*. Berkeley: University of California Press, 1953.

Curtis, Natalie. "Creation Myth of the Cochans (Yuma)." *The Craftsman* 16 (1909): 559-67.

DeArmond, Dale. *The Boy who Found the Light*. San Francisco: Sierra Club Books, 1990.

Dorsey, George A. *Traditions of the Caddo*. Washington, D. C.: Carnegie Institution of Washington, 1905.

Erdoes, Richard, and Alfonso Ortiz, eds. *American Indian Myths and Legends*. New York: Pantheon Books, 1984.

———. *The Sound of Flutes and other Indian Legends*. New York: Pantheon Books, 1976.

Gifford, Edward Winslow, and Gwendoline Harris Block. *Californian Indian Nights Entertainment.* Glendale: Arthur H. Clark Company, 1930.

Huffstetler, Edward W. *Myths of the World: Tales of Native America.* New York: Metro Books, 1996.

Judson, Katharine Berry. *Myths and Legends of British North America.* Chicago: A. C. McClurg & Co. 1917.

——. *Myths and Legends of California and the Old Southwest.* Chicago: A. C. McClurg & Company, 1912.

——. *Myths and Legends of Alaska.* Chicago: A. C. McClurg & Co., 1911.

——. *Myths and Legends of the Pacific Northwest.* Chicago: A. C. McClurg & Co., 1910.

Kroeber, Alfred L. "Cheyenne Tales." *Journal of American Folk-Lore* 13 (1900): 161-90.

Latta, Frank Forrest. *California Indian Folklore.* Self-published, Shafter, California, 1936.

Leeming, David Adam. *Creation Myths of the World: An Encyclopedia.* 2nd ed. Volume 1: Parts I and II. Santa Barbara: ABC-CLIO, 2010.

——, and Jake Page. *The Mythology of Native North America.* Norman: University of Oklahoma Press, 1998.

——, and Margaret Leeming. *A Dictionary of Creation Myths.* Oxford: Oxford University Press, 1994.

Leland, Charles G. *The Algonquin Legends of New England: or, Myths and Folk Lore of the Micmac, Passamaquoddy, and Penobscot Tribes.* Boston: Houghton, Mifflin and Company, 1884.

Malotki, Ekkehart. *Gullible Coyote/Una'ihu: A Bilingual Collection of Hopi Coyote Stories.* Tucson: University of Arizona Press, 1985.

Mayer, Marianna. *Women Warriors: Myths and Legends of Heroic Women.* New York: Morrow Junior Books, 1999.

Mechling, W. H. *Malecite Tales.* Ottawa: Government Printing Bureau, 1914.

Millman, Lawrence. *A Kayak Full of Ghosts.* Santa Barbara: Capra Press, 1987.

Morris, Cora. *Stories from Mythology: North American.* Boston: Marshall Jones Company, 1924.

Powers, Stephen. *Tribes of California.* Contributions to North American Ethnology, vol. 3. Washington, D. C.: Government Printing Office, 1877.

Prince, John Dyneley. *Passamaquoddy Texts.* New York: G. E. Stechert & Co., 1921.

Rasmussen, Knud. *Eskimo Folk-Tales.* Trans. and ed. W. Worster. London: Gylendal, 1921.

Schomp, Virginia. *Myths of the World: The Native Americans.* New York: Marshall Cavendish Benchmark, 2008.

Sekaquaptewa, Emory, and Barbara Pepper, ed. and trans. *Coyote and Little Turtle/Iisaw Niqw Yöngösonhoya: A Traditional Hopi Tale.* Based on a story told by Herschel Talashoema. Santa Fe: Clear Light Publishers, 1994.

Spence, Lewis. *The Myths of the North American Indians.* London: G. Harrap, 1914.

Swann, Brian, ed. *Algonquian Spirit: Contemporary Translations of the Algonquian Literatures of North America.* Lincoln: University of Nebraska Press, 2005.

Teit, James Alexander. *Memoir of the American Museum of Natural History, New York.* Vol. 2, pt. 7: *The Shuswap.* Leiden: E. J. Brill, Ltd., 1909.

Thompson, Stith. *Tales of the North American Indians.* Cambridge, MA: Harvard University Press, 1929.

Tigerman, Kathleen, ed. *Wisconsin Indian Literature: Anthology of Native Voices.* Madison: University of Wisconsin Press, 2006.

Wilson, Gilbert L. *Indian Hero Tales.* New York: American Book Company, 1916.

General Background

Childs, Craig. *Atlas of a Lost World: Travels in Ice Age America.* New York: Pantheon Books, 2018.

Culin, Stewart. "Games of the North American Indians." In *Twenty-Fourth Annual Report of the Bureau of American Ethnology of the Smithsonian Institution,* pp. 1-846. Washington, D. C.: Government Printing Office, 1907.

Gugliotta, Guy. "When Did Humans Come to the Americas?" Smithsonian.com, February 2013. <https://www.smithsonianmag.com/science-nature/when-did-humans-come-to-the-americas-4209273/>.

Worrall, Simon. "When, How Did the First Americans Arrive? It's Complicated." *National Geographic,* 9 June 2018. <https://www.nationalgeographic.com/news/2018/06/when-and-how-did-the-first-americans-arrive--its-complicated-/>.

Printed in Great Britain
by Amazon

26057094R00106